SIMÓN BOLÍVAR

STATUE OF THE LIBERATOR
at the head of the Avenue of the Americas,
New York City.

SIMÓN BOLÍVAR

by
Daniel A. del Río

THE BOLIVARIAN SOCIETY
OF THE UNITED STATES, INC.
1965

All Rights Reserved

Foreword.

I DEDICATE this essay to Mary Washington, my wife, whose patience and understanding during the many months of my research were an inspiration. To Arthur W. Buttenheim, without whose encouragement and Bolivarian zest, this biography would not have been written. And finally, I owe a debt of gratitude to Miss Mariette C. Gilchrist, who corrected the manuscript, greatly helped with her advice in its text and preparation, and whose executive secretarial services were invaluable.

THE AUTHOR

Contents

Introduction.

THIS biography has been written by Mr. Daniel A. del Río so as to make available in English a brief summary of the Great Liberator's life, and is the result of many months of intensive research. The Bolivarian Society of the United States, Inc., has been fortunate in having as one of its active members Mr. del Río, one of the greatest living authorities on the life and heroic deeds of Simón Bolívar.

The biography is being distributed without cost to professors and students of history throughout the U.S.A. This has been made possible through generous contributions from the following:

> American & Foreign Power Company, Inc.
> The Chase Manhattan Bank
> Chemical Bank New York Trust Company
> Continental Bank International
> W. R. Grace & Company
> Manufacturers Hanover Trust Company

It is our hope that as a result this generation may show greater interest in doing everything in their power to preserve for future generations the great heritage of freedom which was passed on to them by the founders of our country.

There seems to be much in common in the life of our own George Washington, North American Liberator, and that of Simón Bolívar, South American Liberator. Both came from fairly wealthy families but endured many periods of hardship during their leadership in battles for freedom; both were reviled by former so-called friends when they most needed support and comfort. One important gift that they had in common was the will and strength of mind and body so that they never gave up or lost their determination to carry through successfully the great causes for which they risked their lives and fortunes.

Simón Bolívar was an inspired and gifted statesman, as well as a military genius. His love for liberty was the driving force which helped him to carry on when others felt that he was beaten.

Let us hope that some day the dream that Bolívar had, of a United America which would embrace the whole of our hemisphere, may become a happy reality.

A. W. BUTTENHEIM,
President of the Bolivarian Society of the United States, Inc.

SIMÓN BOLÍVAR

CHAPTER I

The Early Years

Simón Bolívar* was born in Caracas, Venezuela, on July 24, 1783.

The first of the Bolívars to emigrate to the New World from Spain was his ancestor, Simón Bolívar, related to the most noble families of Biscay. This first ancestor came in 1587 to the recently founded colony of Tierra Firme (now Venezuela) as Secretary to the Governor and Captain General of the Colony, Don Diego de Osorio. Later he acted as Attorney and Royal Commissioner to King Philip II. During the next two centuries, his descendants greatly contributed to the development of the country by helping to build the Port of La Guaira, and numerous roads, and by establishing the agricultural colonies of the Aragua and Tuy Valleys, rich in sugar cane, cocoa and tobacco. Two of these Bolívars acted as Mayors of Caracas, and one of them was appointed Lieutenant Governor of the Colony. In due time the wealth of the Bolívars was considerable as it included, besides extensive plantations, the rich copper mines of Aroa, and vast holdings in the cities.

This brings us to Juan Vicente Bolívar y Ponte, father of the Liberator, who in 1773 married Doña María de la Concepción Palacios y Blanco, also of noble lineage and wealthy in her own right. They had four children, of whom Simón was the youngest. Due to the early death of both his parents (his father died in 1786, when he was three years old, and his mother in 1792, when our future hero was only 9) young Simón spent his

* Baptized on July 30, 1783, as Simón Antonio de la Santísima Trinidad.

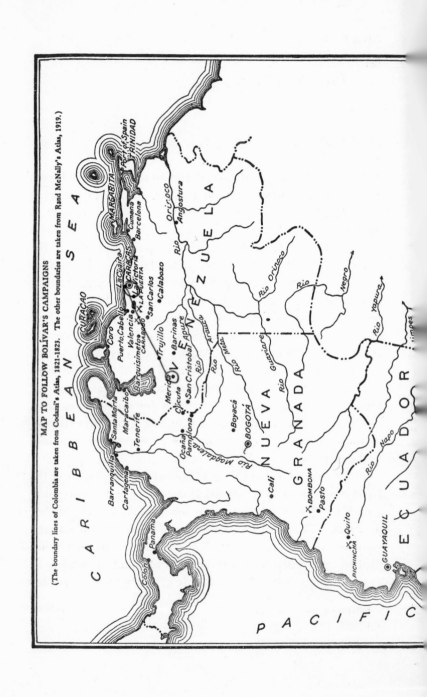

MAP TO FOLLOW BOLIVAR'S CAMPAIGNS

(The boundary lines of Colombia are taken from Codazzi's Atlas, 1821-1823. The other boundaries are taken from Rand McNally's Atlas, 1919.)

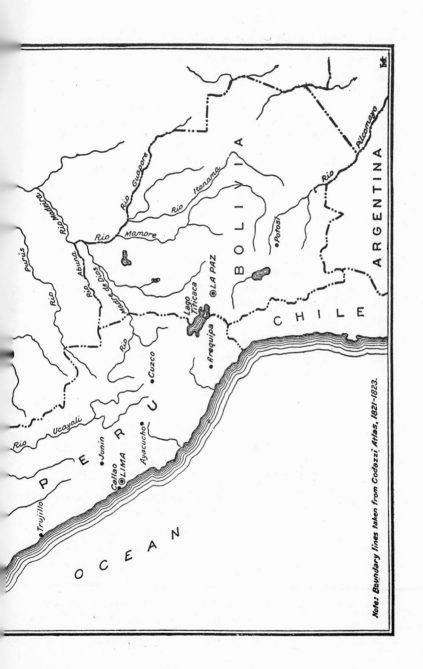

Note: Boundary lines taken from Codazzi Atlas, 1821-1823.

orphaned childhood under the guardianship of his maternal uncle, Carlos Palacios, who took care of Bolívar's extensive properties and provided him with tutors for his education.

Among his early teachers was Andres Bello, only three years his elder, but already an outstanding scholar, who in later years was to become one of the most famous scientists and writers of Spanish America. However, the tutor who was destined to exert the greatest influence in moulding the political philosophy and advanced liberal ideas of the future Liberator, was a young man Simón Rodríguez twelve years older than his pupil, who had recently returned from Europe, and brought fresh to his young disciple the enlightened doctrines of the eighteenth century of the liberal English and French philosophers, particularly those of Jean Jacques Rousseau. Many years later, when Bolívar had assumed the gigantic task of liberating half of the countries of South America, Rousseau's influence on him was as effective as it had been on the men of the French Revolution, and is reflected in his political writings and in the organization of his newly created nations.

But to Rodríguez in conformity with the teachings of Rousseau, the physical development of his pupil was of paramount importance, and during the time when he was at the vast Bolívar plantations, corporal exercises took precedence over everything else. Interminable walks through the fields and surrounding woods horseback riding and swimming filled the daily schedule. As a result of this intensive physical training the future Liberator became an accomplished athlete, excelling in these sports. The Rodríguez tutorship lasted only five years, because in 1797 the teacher returned to Europe.

The next two years were spent by our young Bolívar in the Corps of Cadets of the Aragua Militia where he attained the rank of Lieutenant.

At the beginning of 1799, when Bolívar was sixteen, his

6

guardian Carlos Palacios decided to send him to Spain to broaden his education. While in Madrid he resided for a time in the home of his maternal uncle, Esteban Palacios, but soon went to live at the palace of another relative, the Marquis of Ustáriz. It was here or perhaps while visiting the northern Spanish Provinces, in the summer of 1800, that he met and fell in love at first sight with María Teresa Rodríguez del Toro, several years his elder, niece of the Marquis del Toro of Caracas. After a two-year courtship, during which time he visited Paris, he married her in the spring of 1802. Returning soon after to Caracas with his bride, he had the misfortune* of losing her, ten months later. She succumbed to yellow fever on January 22, 1803.

Six months after the loss of his wife, Bolívar decided to return to Europe. After a short stay in Madrid, he arrived in Paris in the Spring of 1804. On his previous sojourn to the cradle of the French Revolution he had become an admirer of Napoleon, the Consul, whom he considered the hero of the Republic and a pillar of strength. However, when Bolívar visited Paris for the second time, the Empire was established and his previous admiration for Napoleon, the Republican, was shattered. He found monarchy and its flamboyance repugnant. On one occasion he is said to have exclaimed, when referring to Napoleon: "Bonaparte lost a great deal when he became a César.

During his brief stay in Paris, he called almost daily on Baron von Humboldt who, together with his pupil, Aimé Goujand Bonpland had just returned from a five-year scientific expedition throughout Mexico and the northern re-

---

* One hundred years later, a noted South American, commenting on this misfortune and the fact that the Liberator never remarried, said: "Neither Washington nor Bolívar was destined to have any children of his own in order that we Americans might call ourselves their children."

gions of South America. An anecdote relates that during one of these visits Humboldt expressed to Bolívar his deep admiration for the riches of the New World and of its great future if its people could only break the bonds of slavery that chained them to Spain. And then, it is said, Humboldt added: "I believe your country is ripe for that but I do not see the man who could undertake this task."

Bolívar, who up to that time had been living a hollow and purposeless life, that of a wealthy noble scion, partaking of the pleasures of young Paris society, decided there and then to devote all his energies and direct all his future endeavors to the liberation of his country.

It was March, 1805. Napoleon had recently been crowned Emperor. Bolívar, while hating the pomp of royalty, which was contrary to his liberal principles, upon seeing the Emperor acclaimed by the explosion of enthusiasm of over a million people, considered these ovations of the French the uppermost human aspiration, the supreme ambition of man. This recalled to his mind the remark made by Humboldt about Bolívar's country in chains and the glory that would crown its liberator.

That Bolívar admired Napoleon the warrior (although he hated Napoleon the Emperor) is apparent in Bolívar's subsequent military campaigns, in the similarity of his tactics and strategy to Napoleon's concept of war. Bolívar followed the Napoleonic school in his swiftness of action in battle as well as in the grandiloquence and exalted style of his proclamations and addresses to his soldiers. When organizing the governments of the newly liberated nations, Bolívar was inspired by the Napoleonic codes of law. This becomes obvious when one delves into the vast mass of documents and writings of Bolívar and leads to the conclusion that the genius of the Liberator

8

was guided by two masters: Rousseau, the writer-philosopher, and Napoleon, the conqueror and legislator.

It was at this time that Bolívar turned again to his former teacher, Rodríguez, who was then in Vienna. In the Spring of 1805 master and pupil journeyed on foot through the Alps to Italy and visited Rome. While in the Eternal City, in the middle of August, teacher and pupil stood on the summit of Mount Aventino. Below was the Appian Way and beyond the Palatine stood the Forum Romanum with its marble monuments, mute relics of the greatness of Ancient Rome. After a few moments contemplation the young man turned to his tutor and exclaimed:

"I swear before you, I swear by the God of my forefathers, I swear by my native country, that I shall never give rest to my arm nor to my soul until I have broken the shackles which chain us to Spain!"

Twenty years later, after the entire South American Continent had been liberated, a stepson of George Washington arranged for General Lafayette to present to Bolívar a miniature and a medallion, which had belonged to George Washington, with the request that he keep them in memory of the illustrious North American Liberator.

Today, as an aftermath of the Mount Aventino vow of Bolívar, there are many of his statues in the principal cities of the two Americas, including one in Washington and another in New York. Furthermore, several cities in the United States bear the proud name of BOLÍVAR.

Also in 1958 the United States Government in Washington issued in Bolívar's honor a memorial postage stamp, bearing his picture in a medallion, with the inscription:

CHAMPION OF LIBERTY

CHAPTER II

The Baptism of Fire

A FTER a sojourn in Italy of several months, spent by Bolívar and Rodríguez for the most part in visiting the countryside around Naples, during which time Bolívar scaled Mount Vesuvius with Humboldt, they returned to Paris, where teacher and pupil parted company, not to see each other again for another twenty years, when Bolívar was at the height of his glory. Obsessed with a determination to return to Venezuela, the future Liberator set sail for the United States late in 1806 where he visited Boston, New York, Philadelphia and Charleston. In February of 1807 he arrived in Caracas.

During the next three years the Spanish American Colonies were aroused by events in the Peninsula and by the invasion of Spain by Napoleon. The agitation for independence from the mother country started in Caracas. The rejection of José Bonaparte (brother of the Emperor) as King of Spain and the occupation of most of that country by French Armies stirred to action the people of Venezuela. On April 19, 1810 the Colonial Governor, Don Vicente Emparán, was deposed in Caracas, and a Junta (Supreme Conservative Committee of the rights of Ferdinand VII) independent from the French usurper but under the scepter of King Ferdinand VII—the deposed Spanish Monarch—was established.

Bolívar openly supported this movement toward independence and participated in the conspiracy. Two months later, after having been commissioned Lieutenant Colonel in the Militia, he was sent by the Junta to London, with Luís López Méndez as his assistant and Andrés Bello, his former tutor, as secretary, to solicit the protection of the British Government.

The Baptism of Fire

Bolívar was not successful in this, his first diplomatic mission*, because England, although at heart sympathetic with his ideas of liberation, was allied at the time with Spain against Bonaparte and was reluctant to openly help gain the independence of colonies belonging to its Ally.

It was due to this official mission that the public life of the future Liberator in the service of his country actually began and was to continue for the next twenty years, until his death in 1830. While in London Bolívar spent his spare time in the study of the British Parliament and its Constitution which he greatly admired. He then and there resolved that if he had any part in the shaping of his country's form of government he would initiate in Venezuela some of these British principles, adopting them with such modifications as the differences in climate, customs and race made desirable and possible.

In London, Bolívar succeeded in persuading General Francisco de Miranda**, who was then living there, to return to

* At Apsley House, the Duke of Wellington's residence in London, there is a bronze plaque with the following inscription:

"In honor of Simón Bolívar, the Liberator, who as first accredited Spanish American Representative was received in this house by the marquess of Wellesley, His Majesty's principal Secretary of State for Foreign Affairs, on July 17, 1810."

** General Francisco de Miranda, born in Caracas on March 28, 1750, was the harbinger of the liberation of the Spanish Colonies in South America. At an early age he migrated to Europe where he began to preach the gospel of independence for Spanish America. Miranda, with the rank of Lieutenant General, fought in the armies of the French Revolution, and his name is engraved in the Arc de Triomphe in Paris. He died on July 14, 1816 in Cádiz, a prisoner of the Spaniards. Miranda designed the present flag, adopted by Colombia, Venezuela and Ecuador as their national emblem. Among the many anecdotes concerning the colors of the flag it is narrated that Miranda added to the colors of the Spanish flag, namely gold and scarlet, a blue stripe, the color he had seen Washington adopt for the Order of the Cincinnati. Miranda was also responsible for giving the name of COLOMBIA to part of the territories comprising then TIERRA FIRME, which was done in homage to the discoverer of America.

Venezuela and help in consolidating the country's independence. Bolívar returned to Caracas on December 5, 1810, and Miranda arrived several days later.

A few days before the return of Bolívar to Venezuela, two of the Venezuelan Provinces, Maracaibo and Coro, which had refused to join the Caracas patriots in their bid for independence, openly revolted against the Central Junta. The latter decided to send a contingent of about 4000 men under General Marquis del Toro (November 28, 1810) to bring them into submission. Unfortunately, these hastily cashiered and ill-equipped troops were repulsed, with great losses, before the City of Coro, defended by the Spanish Governor of that province, Don Fernando Miyares, later appointed Captain General of Caracas.

These were some of the headaches confronting the Caracas Junta when Bolívar returned from his unsuccessful London Mission. As his reception by the patriots was rather cold, he decided to retire to his plantations to hide his disappointment. Miranda's reception was similarly far from enthusiastic but he succeeded, after a few months, in being elected a member of the Congress that met for the first time on March 2, 1811, as one of the Representatives from the Province of Barcelona. This Congress as constituted included seven of the Federated Provinces of Venezuela, namely: Caracas, Cumaná, Barcelona, Margarita, Barinas, Mérida and Trujillo. On July 5, 1811 it proclaimed its independence from Spain.

As the forces of the patriots under Marquis del Toro were unable to stifle the revolt, General Miranda was appointed to replace him. When Miranda accepted the command of the troops, he stipulated as one of his conditions that Bolívar was to be excluded from serving in the army. The reason for this was that since the return of both patriots to Venezuela serious differences of opinion had arisen between them.

12

Bolívar, up to the time of his mission to London, had admired Miranda and considered him as possibly that providential leader who could liberate his country, who Humboldt had said did not exist. However, he soon discovered that his idol, who was thirtythree years his senior, possibly because of his long residence in Europe, found it difficult to adjust to his new surroundings, was critical in his appraisal of the problems confronting the patriots, and was utterly indecisive in the field of action. In the eyes of Bolívar, Miranda lacked military perseverance, a quality without which—and independent of Miranda's great personal courage—no great military undertakings could be successfully completed. Miranda, on the other hand, considered Bolívar a dangerous, impulsive and inexperienced young man. However, because of the seriousness of the military situation confronting them, they soon patched up their differences and Bolívar was allowed to join the Miranda forces as Lieutenant Colonel of a battalion.

The army of the patriots, after two days of ferocious hand to hand combat, succeeded in retaking Valencia (August 13, 1811). In this action Bolívar distinguished himself for his fearlessness in leading his battalion to victory. As a reward, Miranda recommended his promotion to full Colonel and sent him to Caracas to bring to the Congress the glad tidings of the fall of Valencia. The daring and superb strategy displayed by Bolívar in leading his men to victory at Valencia, against great odds, not only endeared him to his young lieutenants but was the beginning of that admiration and loyalty, almost bordering on worship, which his troops felt for him, whether in fortune or adversity, that was to continue for the next eighteen years, until his death. Valencia was his first experience in combat, the baptism of fire of the future Liberator. He was then twentyeight years old.

A few months later, on December 21, 1811, the Congress assembled at Caracas promulgated the Venezuelan Constitution, and named Valencia the seat of the Confederation, where the next meeting of the legislators was to take place. However, the Royal Commissioner of Spain, Governor Fernando Miyares, from his seat of government in Coro was not idle. Taking advantage of the arrival in Coro from Puerto Rico of some troop reinforcements under the command of Frigate Captain Domingo Monteverde, Miyares decided to send Monteverde with 500 soldiers to subdue Siquisaque, a small town on the road to Barquisimeto. Monteverde was victorious not only there but also at nearby Carora, where he succeeded in increasing his forces tenfold, and then marched against Barquisimeto, where Miranda was encamped with a contingent of troops far superior to those of Monteverde.

At this juncture occurred one of the greatest national disasters that ever afflicted Venezuela: the earthquake* of March 26, 1812, when the patriot cities of Caracas, La Guaira, Barquisimeto and Mérida were destroyed, while the royalist cities of Valencia, Puerto Cabello, Coro and Maracaibo were spared. Over 3000 persons perished.

It is narrated that in Caracas at San Jacinto Square, which had been totally destroyed by the earthquake, a fanatic royalist priest was preaching to the scared populace, perched on the debris of the ruined buildings, saying that "this commotion of nature had descended as a punishment from Heaven to the enemies of the Spanish King." Bolívar who was present, jumping onto the makeshift pulpit, and brushing the monk aside, succeeded, with an impassioned speech, in calming the people, ending his remarks with these words: "If Nature opposes us, we will fight her!—and make her obey us!"

Note: When the extent of the disaster of the Caracas earthquake became known in Washington, the United States Congress decreed the sending to Venezuela of five vessels loaded with flour. Venezuela never forgot this generosity—one of the most noble acts of the American Continent.

The earthquake opened the doors of Barquisimeto and other cities to Monteverde, and six weeks later, after taking the City of San Carlos, he entered with his troops in triumph into Valencia. Confronted with this series of military disasters, Congress appointed Miranda as Dictator and Generalissimo of the Land and Sea Forces of Venezuela (April 26th).

Almost at the same time that Monteverde was entering Valencia, Bolívar had been sent by Miranda to Puerto Cabello to try to save that fortress city from the menacing Spanish forces. However, his small garrison was unable to withstand the repeated onslaughts of an enemy several times stronger, and after two months of heroic defense, he suffered the loss of the forts, due to the treason of one of his Lieutenants, Francisco Fernandez Vinoni,* who delivered them to the enemy. Bolívar escaped with a few faithful officers to La Guaira, while Monteverde, after taking Puerto Cabello, compelled Miranda to capitulate. The first Republic of Venezuela had ceased to exist.

The surrender signed by Miranda, which meant the dissolution of the army and the abandonment of all their immediate hopes for liberty, was ill-received by the patriots, including Bolívar, who resolved to emigrate rather than submit forever again to the Spanish rule. To make matters worse, Monteverde, after entering Caracas, violated the articles of the capitulation and permitted his troops to commit all kinds of excesses, ransacking the defenseless towns and massacring its helpless inhabitants. Miranda, finding himself in great danger of being taken prisoner by the enemy, decided that he had no choice but to try to escape the country. He arrived at La Guaira on July 30, 1812. That night a council of officers, including Bolí-

---

* Seven years later, after the battle of Boyaca, which liberated Colombia (Nueva Granada) Bolívar recognized Vinoni, the traitor, among the prisoners then taken and had him hanged from a tree, on the spot.

var, declared Miranda a traitor, and next morning he was imprisoned and delivered to the Spanish authorities. Miranda died four years later, on July 14, 1816, in a Cadiz dungeon, chained to the walls like a dog. His remains have never been found.

In spite of his mistakes, Miranda was a great patriot deserving a better fate. His genius conceived for the first time the future of a South America, free and independent. He was a martyr to this cause. At the Pantheon in Caracas, where Bolívar and his generals are buried, there is a beautiful marble monument, shaped like a coffin, with the lid held half-open by a majestic eagle, waiting for his remains. And if Venezuela never forgot him, France perpetuated his memory by engraving prominently his name among 386 heroes of the French Revolution, in the Arc de Triomphe in Paris.

After the delivery of Miranda to the Spaniards, Bolívar, having lost all of his properties, which had been confiscated by Monteverde, was able to leave the country only through the intercession of a Spanish friend of his family, Francisco Iturbe. He arrived in Curacao on September 9, 1812, and several weeks later sailed for Cartagena, a Province of Nueva Granada* (Colombia) which in October of that year had joined the other provinces of Nueva Granada, proclaiming its absolute independence from Spain.

Here ends that part of the life of our hero, during which he received his baptism of fire under Miranda. It was in this period of time that his mind became focussed on the great goals to which he was going to devote his future efforts as a unique leader, as the Liberator not only of his own native country but of the entire South American Continent.

* Conquistador Gonzalo Jiménez de Quesada, founder of Santa Fé de Bogotá, was born in the Spanish village of Santa Fé, Kingdom of Granada. He named the territory he had conquered: "Nueva Granada."

CHAPTER III

The Admirable Campaign

B OLÍVAR was warmly and generously received by the Government of Cartagena. Immediately upon his arrival he issued a proclamation explaining the atrocities committed by Monteverde in Venezuela, ending with these words:

"AMERICANS; Let us no longer be the object of the sarcasm of those wretched Spaniards who are superior to us only in wickedness, while they do not excel us in valor, because our indulgence is what gives them their strength. If they appear great to us, it is because we are on our knees. Let us avenge three centuries of shame. War alone can only save us through the path of honor!"

This was followed on December 15, 1812 by his famous public declaration (Manifesto of Cartagena) considered a monument of military and political dialectics, in which he explains the causes for the loss of Venezuela and how, in order for the patriots to overcome their enemies it was essential that they should establish a strong central government, apply the entire resources of the State to the war, have veteran armies, and always be on the offensive. In this declaration Bolívar's purpose was to arouse the citizens of Nueva Granada (Colombia) and of Cartagena to the necessity of uniting all of the peoples of Spanish America against the common enemy and obtaining from them assistance to liberate his country. Concerning the causes of the defeat of the first Republic of Venezuela, he said in part:

"The codes consulted by our Magistrates were not those which could teach them the practical science of Government but were those devised by certain benevolent visionaries, who, creating fantastic republics in their imaginations, have sought to attain political perfection, assuming the perfectibility of the human race. Thus we were given philosophers for leaders, philanthropy for legislation, dialectic for tactics, and sophists for soldiers!"

As regards the direction of the war, the future Liberator stressed the Napoleonic principle of the advantages of war carried out with strategy and audacity, emphasizing that if the resources of one of the provinces were sufficient to conquer Venezuela, with those of the entire Venezuela all of the Spanish colonies could be liberated. He said: "Coro is to Caracas as Caracas is to all America." * And then he thus added:

"Let us hasten to break the chains of those victims who groan in the dungeons, ever hopeful of rescue. Do not betray their confidence. Do not be insensible to the cries of your brothers. Fly to avenge the dead, to give life to the dying, to bring freedom to the oppressed and liberty to all!"

Bolívar carried into practice these lofty principles, which on the surface seemed the illusions of a feverish imagination. From Cartagena he went in triumph to Caracas, and when for the second and third times he was forced to leave the country (see Chapters IV and V) after two years of conflict against the popular resistance of the people to be liberated, he returned with a handful of followers in a triumphal march, that

* He referred to Monteverde who, with scanty resources from the small province of Coro and a handful of men, had succeeded in a few months in subjugating all of Venezuela.

took him and his victorious army from the scorching beaches of the Orinoco River on the Atlantic to the frigid peaks of the Andes of Potosí on the Pacific.

Notwithstanding the importance of the above proclamation, Bolívar was given only the appointment of commandant of the insignificant post of Barranca, a small port of the Magdalena River, garrisoned with 70 men. From here Bolívar, who succeeded in increasing his forces to about 250, took Tenerife, a river fort manned by royalists, and also destroyed various Spanish garrisons at Guamal, Banco, Chiriguaná, Tamalameque and Puerto Real, opening again, through the river, the communications of Cartagena with the interior provinces. This campaign was the beginning of another even more important one. With reinforcements by volunteers from Mompox, Cartagena, and Bogotá, he directed his efforts to his dream of redeeming Caracas, the cradle of the South American independence.

At the beginning of 1813 he occupied Ocaña and through brilliant strategy he succeeded in defeating enemy forces several times superior in numbers and in taking the important Colombian border City of Cúcuta, in February. His small number of followers had now been increased to 450, whereas the Spaniards were 1300 strong. At Cúcuta the doors of Venezuela were opened to the audacious invaders. Having crossed the border to the Venezuelan town of San Antonio, Bolívar there issued on March 1, 1813 a proclamation to his soldiers, which ended as follows:

"In less than two months you have carried out two campaigns and have started a third one, that begins here and which must end in the country which gave me life!

"America expects its liberation and salvation from you, soldiers of Cartagena and of the Union. Fly to cover yourselves with glory, winning the sublime name of Liberators of Venezuela!"

Bolívar invaded Venezuela with a handful of young officers, among which were many who later received the greatest honors that history can bestow. Five of them deserve special mention: *Born in Nueva Granada:* Atanasio Girardot, Antonio Ricaurte, Joaquín París. *Born in Venezuela:* Rafael Urdaneta, José Félix Ribas. The oldest was Ribas, 37 years old. All of the others, except Urdaneta, who at the time was 23, were under 22 years of age.

The opposition of some of his subordinates to his plan to invade Venezuela ceased when in May 1813 he received approval to his project from the Presidents of Nueva Granada and Cundinamarca, but limiting it to the liberation of two Venezuelan Provinces: Mérida and Trujillo. After receiving this authorization Bolívar invaded Venezuela on May 14th and scarcely one week later, May 23rd, he arrived with the vanguard of his small forces at Mérida. It was here that he was proclaimed: LIBERATOR!

While at Mérida, Bolívar persisted in his plan to reach Caracas, and so wrote on May 26, 1813, to the Nueva Granada President, ending with this prophecy:

"Within two months we will see fully liberated the Republic of Venezuela, provided the Supreme Executive Power authorizes me to act according to circumstances." *

Bolívar's prophecy was fulfilled because two months and a half after leaving Mérida, he triumphantly entered Caracas,

---

* This authorization was granted and was received by Bolívar at Trujillo in June 1813. It had the limitation that three commissioners, being sent by the Central Government of Nueva Granada, were to approve in case of need the decisions of the Commander in Chief.

on August 6, 1813. Bolívar left Mérida on May 26th. To narrate in full the fascinating and triumphant march of the Liberator from this city to Caracas would require the space of a full-sized volume. This we are unable to do, due to the abridged nature of this biography. But we cannot refrain from mentioning here that in the annals of the world's great military undertakings, one of the most amazing for its audacity, swiftness of action, superb tactics and unmatched strategy is this, so properly called, ADMIRABLE CAMPAIGN of Bolívar. In the short period of a little over two months, he covered a distance (on horseback, but his troops mostly on foot) of nearly 500 miles between Mérida and Caracas, which actually was twice that distance because of his marches and counter-marches and detours in order to take by surprise an enemy five to ten times stronger. During this time he fought six major battles and a number of important combats.

His daring, in engaging in battle the Spanish contingents, so superior in numbers, who were waiting strategically entrenched at the various cities on the way to Caracas, was unmatched. In his tactics he followed those of Napoleon in fighting the enemy piecemeal, attacking swiftly when least expected, sometimes from the rear. This gradual annihilation of the Spanish forces in isolated groups, effectively prevented the enemy from concentrating their widely scattered forces into a more compact and formidable gathering of troops, as was the plan of the Spanish generals.

The gigantic task of the Liberator in this campaign was overwhelming. His small contingent of troops when he left Mérida, consisting of about 700 men, was almost destitute of the essentials in equipment and weapons considered necessary to fight well-trained and organized forces as those of the enemy. Furthermore, his handful of soldiers, consisting mostly of volunteers from the scorching tropical lowlands, were unaccustomed to the frigid climate of the Mérida Sierras, which they had to cross and crisscross in marches and countermarches, sometimes at altitudes of over 13,000 feet. This was an epic comparable only to the crossing of the Alps by Hannibal or Bonaparte, although the Alps are much lower.

In the forced trek through the rocky and formidable canyons and in the inhospitable highlands of the mighty Venezuelan Andes, the morale of the troops, notwithstanding their tremendous hardships, was superb, due to the unmatched leadership of Bolívar.

After taking the important city of Trujillo, situated about one fourth of the way between Mérida and Caracas, Bolívar was compelled to issue his famous proclamation "WAR TO THE DEATH," considered by Baralt as the greatest and most transcendental of his revolutionary thoughts, which ended with these redoubtable words:

"SPANIARDS AND CANARIANS:* you will be shot even if found innocent if you do not take an active part on behalf of the freedom of the Americas. AMERICANS:** Your life will be spared, even if you are found guilty. —Trujillo, June 15, 1813."

To crush the incipient revolt of the native population against their oppressors, the Spanish armies in Venezuela had resorted to terror and mass slaughter. No prisoners were taken. When the Spanish armies entered a town that had taken sides with the patriots, its hapless inhabitants were massacred, the women raped, and the buildings looted and totally

* *Canarians:* Natives of the Spanish Canary Islands, situated on the northwest coast of Africa, facing Southern Morocco and Spanish Sahara.

** *Americans:* Many of the native South Americans in the Spanish Army had been conscripted and compelled to fight the forces of the Liberator, who, therefore, decreed that their lives would be spared if they were captured.

destroyed. Torture of its leaders by cutting off their ears, cheeks and noses, was followed by their being drawn and quartered. As Bolívar failed in his efforts to have the Spanish Generals end this savagery, he was forced, notwithstanding his most lofty humanitarian principles, to issue the above "WAR TO THE DEATH" proclamation.

At Trujillo, before proceeding north to San Carlos, his next goal on the road to Caracas, Bolívar decided first to take the City of Barinas, the gateway to the Venezuelan plains, about 75 miles in direct line to the southwest, where the largest concentration of troops of the enemy, 1500 strong, was entrenched. He did not want to continue north and leave these Spanish contingents menacing his rear.

Personally leading his small force of soldiers, about one third of that of the enemy numerically, Bolívar executed one of his brilliant maneuvers of the campaign. Instead of following the straight route of the mountain canyons, abrupt and difficult, between Trujillo and Barinas, which was the direction the enemy expected him to take, he decided to deceive them. By making a detour of 120 miles to the northeast, through the Boconó Valley and the mountain pass to Guanare, crossing the Andes at an altitude of 11,000 feet, he placed himself and his troops between the rear of the Spaniards at Barinas and Caracas, effectively cutting off their communications with that city, and thus preventing them from receiving any reinforcements. However, his main purpose was to attack the enemy unexpectedly from the rear. The Spaniards, taken by surprise, abandoned the city, practically without firing a shot.

On another occasion, at the decisive battle of Taguanes, where the Bolívar contingents had by then been increased to about 1600 troops, the Liberator, perceiving that the enemy, 2000 strong, did not want to engage in battle and was escaping to join other forces in the north, ordered an infantry battalion to pursue, mounted on the rumps of the horses of a squadron of cavalry. These troops, moving swiftly in a parallel line, ahead of the enemy, upon reaching the foothills of the sierra, dismounted and attacked the vanguard of the Spaniards, while other Bolívar infantry columns were breaking their rearguard. The enemy surrendered en masse, and its General, critically wounded, died that night.

One week after the Taguanes victory, Bolívar occupied Valencia and then entered Caracas, on August 6, 1813. Monteverde, who up to then had been Captain General of Venezuela, having lost everything, escaped with a contingent of 250 soldiers and took refuge at the fortress city of Puerto Cabello.

It was at Caracas, at the height of his glory, that our hero who had sacrificed his great wealth and abandoned everything in life to serve his country, made his first public declaration by which the world could know he had no personal ambition. A proclamation he issued to the inhabitants of Caracas, on August 9, 1813, ended as follows:

"The Liberator of Venezuela renounces forever and declines irrevocably to accept any office except the post of danger at the head of our soldiers in defense of the salvation of our country."

This was to be his Code of Honor until his death, seventeen years later. Whether leading his troops to victory or as President of Colombia, he never personally benefitted from any remuneration. And when Peru, in gratitude for its liberation, decreed a million soles* to him, he refused to accept the gift.

* (Then equivalent to One Million Dollars.)

CHAPTER IV

Defeat and Exile

A LMOST at the same time that Bolívar was marching in triumph from Mérida to Caracas, a group of young patriots led by General Santiago Mariño* among which were the two Bermúdez brothers, Manuel Piar, Manuel Valdez, Antonio José de Sucre and many others, 45 in all in the group, succeeded in liberating the eastern part of Venezuela, achieving glorious victories crowned by the taking of the important eastern city of Cumaná, four days before Bolívar entered Caracas.

Mariño and his young companions had taken refuge in the British Island of Trinidad, from where they later invaded eastern Venezuela. While at Trinidad, Sir Ralph Woodford, Governor of the island, was rather unfriendly to these refugees and spared no effort in causing them all forms of inconveniences. One one occasion, he addressed a letter to Mariño as follows: "To Santiago Mariño, General of the Insurgents of Costa Firme" (Venezuela).

Mariño, who was a great patriot with a violent temper, answered Woodford as follows:

"Whatever may have been the intentions of Your Excellency in calling me an insurgent, I am far from considering such an epithet a dishonor when I remember that the British called Washington by the same name."

The triumph of the patriots was opportune because it coincided with great happenings on the Iberic Peninsula which were to exert a decisive influence in favor of the King among

* Mariño was born at Margarita in 1788 and died at La Victoria on September 4, 1854.

the Spanish American Colonies. The day Bolívar entered Mérida the French Armies evacuated Madrid, and the capture of Caracas was accomplished when Napoleon's armies were abandoning the Spanish territory, due to their defeat by Wellington at Vitoria.

However, the inhabitants of Venezuela, accustomed to 300 years of royal reign, were ill-prepared to adapt themselves to the new republican order. Besides, the changed political system resulted in the loss of property and the partisans of the royalist cause were soon aware that the patriots lacked sufficient troops and weapons to defend themselves. Furthermore, the victories of Spain against the French, which confirmed the resurgence of the mother country as a military power, incited the people to rebellion against that handful of men considered visionaries who had assumed power without any right, according to the general popular feelings.

This animosity was aggravated by the jealousy of the middle classes as well as by the feelings of the mulattoes and negroes against the creoles and against the native white descendents of the first Spanish settlers. As soon as the villages and towns in the interior realized the inadequacy of the forces of the liberators, rebellions exploded everywhere and fighting on a large scale was soon to be resumed, submerging the country in a bath of blood that was to continue unabated for the next eight years.

Meanwhile Bolívar, during his short sojourn in Caracas, devoted a great deal of his attention to the reorganization of the State, a gigantic task due to the complete lack of resources resulting from the great political upheaval of the country. In his undertaking he was ably seconded by Dr. Cristóbal Mendoza* in his character of political Governor of the Province.

* Dr. Cristóbal Mendoza: Born in Trujillo in 1772. Died in Caracas 1829. Emigrated to Nueva Granada after the fall of Miranda. Appointed by

In addition to this, the military problems confronting him were overwhelming. In his swift and triumphal march toward Caracas, Bolívar had had no means or the time to consolidate his conquests. Although he had succeeded in destroying the principal enemy forces and had liberated the towns and cities in his path on the way to the Capital, there yet remained in those liberated regions large numbers of enemies of the independence, who were only waiting for an opportune moment to act. Besides, the limited numbers of the liberating troops had not permitted Bolívar to garrison properly the Provinces of Mérida and Trujillo, leaving them exposed to the forays of Spanish General Miyares, Governor of the royalist province of Maracaibo. Likewise, the royalist Province of Coro threatened Barquisimeto, the key to eastern Venezuela; and Spanish Colonel Yáñez, from the Apure plains, constituted a danger to the Province of Barinas. All of the regions of the Tuy Valleys and of the Llanos (plains or savannahs) were replete with elements hostile to the patriots.

One of the military preoccupations that Bolívar tackled upon his arrival in Caracas was Puerto Cabello, where Monteverde was fortified with a handful of soldiers. However, the arrival from Spain of reinforcements consisting of 1200 troops, frustrated Bolívar's original plan of attack, although he succeeded in defeating the detachments led by Monteverde from Puerto Cabello at Bárbula and at Las Trincheras. At Bárbula, Bolívar suffered the loss of one of his best lieutenants, Atanasio Girardot; while at Las Trincheras Monteverde was seriously wounded by a bullet which badly shattered his jaw. Monteverde again took refuge at Puerto Cabello, where on October 28, 1813 he was deposed as Captain General. Two months

---

Bolívar Governor of Mérida and later of Caracas. Fought with great intensity the separatist movement of General Páez. A great patriot with a sterling character.

later he left for Curacao never again to return to Venezuela.

Bolívar carried the heart of Girardot in an urn to be buried with great pomp and high military honors at the Caracas Cathedral. It was at this juncture that he created the "ORDER OF THE LIBERATORS," consisting of a star with seven points (for the seven provinces of Venezuela) and with the legend: "Liberator of Venezuela." The first to receive this decoration were his young lieutenants who had participated in the "Admirable Campaign": Ribas, Urdaneta, D'Elhuyar, Campo Elías, Ortega and others. He also sent a decoration to General Mariño as head of the Eastern Provinces.

However, he soon had to leave Caracas for the western part of the country menaced by Spanish forces from Coro and Maracaibo. At Barquisimeto, at the moment when he thought he had victory within his grasp, he was defeated due to the timidity of a patriot battalion, consisting mostly of green draftees, which he promptly degraded before the remainder of his battered troops. This battalion was to carry the stigma of being called "NAMELESS BATTALION," until it rehabilitated itself by bravery in battle. Less than a month later, on December 15, 1813, at the Battle of Araure won by Bolívar leading his troops in person the battalion as a reward for its gallantry under fire was honored with the name "VENCEDOR EN ARAURE" (Conqueror at Araure).

One of the worst dangers confronting Bolívar was the appearance on the "llanos" (Venezuelan plains) of bands of marauders (llaneros) who, like the ancient barbarians, invaders of Italy and Greece, led by Spaniards or Canarians of the lowest caste, were to plunge the country into a bath of blood and destruction. From the beginning of the revolution these semi-savage "llaneros" (plainsmen) proclaimed themselves for Spain. But their allegiance to the king was a hollow tenet, as was also to them the gospel of independence preached by Bolívar, because in their primitive way they blindly followed their leaders without regard to the side on which they were fighting. These half-naked cowboys from the scorching tropical plains of the Apure, superb horsemen, lawless, submitting to no one except their immediate leaders, ferocious as tigers and expert with the lance, were half-breeds (mestizos), browns, slaves, or descendents of slaves, and constituted a formidable enemy in combat. They had had the good fortune of finding a leader, José Tomás Boves, who had traits similar to theirs—merciless, brutal and bloodthirsty, but equipped with the audacity and skill to lead them in their efforts of conquest.

Boves was a Spaniard born in Asturias in 1782, one year older than Bolívar, who had come to Venezuela as a sailor, was indicted as a pirate and a smuggler, and had been subsequently exiled to the Apure plains, where at the start of the revolution, heading a small group of criminals, he began plundering and terrorizing the hapless hamlets and small villages of those regions. His zeal in killing patriots and subjugating the people of the plains through terror and wholesale murder attracted the attention of Monteverde, who rewarded him with the appointment as Commandant of Calabozo at the beginning of 1813. A year later, at the head of 7000 llaneros, he became master of the vast territories south of Caracas, after exterminating with his hordes every village or town that stood in his path. He never took any prisoners but killed every man, woman and child. During the nearly three years of Boves's depredations possibly one hundred thousand persons perished at his hands or those of his lieutenants. Boves was finally killed while attacking the patriots at the head of his llaneros, at the battle of Urica, on September 12, 1814. Thus perished the worst monster of the wars of independence. *Boves*

As the year 1813 ended with new and threatening clouds

of insurrection menacing the young Republic, the political Governor of Caracas, Dr. Cristóbal Mendoza, on January 2, 1814, at a meeting of the most notable citizens of the city, held at the Convent of San Francisco, conferred upon Bolívar the powers of Dictator to enable him to cope with the mountain of problems confronting the country. Bolívar accepted this new burden with great aversion, ending his speech with these words:

> "My only aspiration is that of continuing to fight your enemies, and I will never sheathe my sword until the freedom of my country is completely assured."

Never was a promise better fulfilled!

However, the year 1814 was going to be one of the blackest and most trying in the annals of Venezuela and of its Liberator. Before the year was over, after many frustrations, great disappointments and military disasters, Bolívar was to taste for the second time the bitterness of exile, leaving the country helpless and submerged in a bath of blood at the hands of its enemies.

When his lieutenants and troops, after a military disaster, considered everything lost, the genius of Bolívar, superior to all human concept, was always able to recreate resources where there were none, and by swiftly reorganizing his shattered forces, again to face the enemy undaunted and stronger than before. The Spanish generals, and among them, General Morillo, frequently said that Bolívar was more to be dreaded after defeat than when victorious. This will of iron and almost superhuman tenacity of the Liberator, as will be seen in the following chapters, was responsible, when he returned to Venezuela for the second and third times, for its liberation and for the liberation from the domination by Spain of all her colonies in the South American continent—this time forever.

During 1814 a total of 65 combats, sieges and battles took place in Venezuela. Bolívar was able to lead his troops in person in only eight of these because of his other manifold duties in reorganizing the government of the new nation. Although his able lieutenants succeeded in winning more than two-thirds of these engagements, disaster soon followed. At the battle of La Puerta, on June 15, 1814, Bolívar with only 3500 troops suffered one of his worst defeats at the hands of Boves leading 8000 llaneros. Over 1000 dead were left strewn over the battlefield. Bolívar and Mariño (who had joined the Liberator two months before) escaped to Caracas with the remnants of their shattered forces, consisting of 400 men.

After his victory Boves entered Valencia and put to the sword everyone known to have supported the patriots. The massacre of the hapless inhabitants of Valencia at the hands of Boves was so brutal that when the news reached Caracas that the Boves hordes were approaching the capital, a great migration of its population toward eastern Venezuela ensued.

Bolívar left with them for Barcelona, protecting with his handful of troops the rearguard of the migration. Of the 40,000 inhabitants of Caracas there remained in the city only about half. Of the half that left, it is said, over ten thousand perished in their trek of twenty days through the deserts and rigorous mountains, through hunger, fatigue and untold privations. This tragic exodus has never been forgotten in Venezuela and can be compared only with the catastrophe caused by the earthquake in 1812.

On his way to Barcelona the Liberator suffered a second and worse defeat at the hands of Morales, the ferocious lieutenant of Boves, who at the head of nearly 8000 llaneros completely shattered Bolivar's small army. The savagery of the hand to hand combat and the heroic resistance of the patriots in defending every inch of ground to the end resulted in 5000 casualties. According to the foremost biographer of Bolívar, Dr. Vicente Lecuna the battle was the bloodiest of the war. The Spaniards beheaded all of the wounded patriots, plus a large number of civilians that had taken refuge in Barcelona. The wounded, the women, the sick, the old people and the children were all massacred, even inside the cathedral where they thought themselves safe. The church soon became a morass of blood and corpses. The patriots losses at the battle, together with the civilians thus executed, were 3700; while the royalists' losses were only 1000. Besides, of the 800 Spaniards wounded in the battlefield, many are said to have died later.

This crushing defeat gave the "coup de grace" to the agonizing remnants of the Republic. Bolívar, together with General Mariño and a handful of followers, escaped to Barcelona, then to Cumaná and Carúpano. When they arrived at this last port city they found that the small garrison of troops of patriots stationed there, incited against the defeated Liberator by Generals José Felix Ribas and Manuel Piar, had revolted, refused to recognize the authority of their former leaders (Bolívar and Mariño) and had appointed Ribas and Piar as their new commanders. Ribas assumed the pompous title of "Supreme Chief of the West" while Piar that of "Supreme Chief of the East."

Having lost everything except his determination and faith in his ability to save his country, Bolívar set sail from Carúpano on board the schooner "El Arrogante" for Cartagena. He was accompanied by Mariño and a handful of faithful officers. Eventually both Ribas and Piar came to a violent end. Scarcely three months after their treachery, Ribas was taken prisoner at Tucupido, subsequently executed by the Spaniards and his head, which had been fried in oil, was sent to Caracas, where it was exhibited inside an iron cage at the entrance to the city until 1817. Piar, a mulatto born in the Island of Curacao in 1782, three years later, on October 16, 1817, after inciting rebellion against Bolívar for the second time, was ordered shot as a traitor by a military tribunal of the patriots in the city of Angostura.

Before leaving Venezuela, the Liberator issued at Carúpano, on September 7, 1814, a proclamation which ended as follows:

"I swear, dear countrymen, that this august title that your gratitude conferred upon me when I came to break your shackles will not be in vain. I swear that Liberator or dead, I will always deserve the honor that you have bestowed upon me. There is no human power on earth that can deter me from the path that I am determined to follow. . . . God awards victory to constancy!"

CHAPTER V

Trials and Tribulations

B OLÍVAR, accompanied by General Mariño and a handful of officers, arrived at Cartagena on September 25, 1814. From there he proceeded to Tunja, in the interior, temporary seat of the Nueva Granada Congress, at which time Santa Fé, (Bogotá) the Capital of the Province of Cundinamarca and the principal city of the country, had refused to recognize the authority of the Central Government. When he appeared before the Congress to render an account of his Venezuelan campaign, its President answered him as follows:

"Your country is not vanquished while your sword exists. General, you, with the sword will again rescue her from the power of her aggressors. The Congress of Nueva Granada will give you its protection because it is satisfied with your conduct. You have been an unfortunate General, but you are a great man."

The government appointed Bolívar General in Chief of the Armies of the Union. His first assignment was to bring Cundinamarca back into the fold of the Federation, which he accomplished after entering Bogotá on December 12, 1814. From there he proceeded to the coast, with instructions to subdue the Provinces of Santa Marta, Río Hacha and Maracaibo. Cartagena had received orders to supply his army with additional guns and ammunition but chose to act independently from the Central Government and refused to comply with this request. Bolívar, rather than lead his army into a civil fratricidal war against Cartagena, which in the past had been for him a second fatherland, chose instead to exile himself. Upon resigning his command, he thus addressed his former officers and soldiers:

"From you, who have been my comrades in innumerable vicissitudes and combats; from you, I part to go and live in exile and idleness instead of dying for my country. But you, who are the judges of my grief, can decide if I am not making the sacrifice of my heart, of my fortune, and of my glory when I give up the honor of leading you to victory. The salvation of the army has imposed this duty upon me. I have not hesitated."

Meanwhile, the King of Spain, Ferdinand VII, who a year before had been returned to the throne and was governing the country as an absolute dictator, sent to the New World an expedition under the command of General Pablo Morillo to bring back its colonies under royal domain. This expedition consisted of 10,500 excellently equipped veteran troops. Morillo's men first landed at the Island of Margarita (facing the eastern provinces of Venezuela) and then entered Caracas, almost at the same time that Bolívar was leaving Cartagena for Jamaica. Morillo, after leaving in Venezuela a garrison of 5500 of his Spanish troops, proceeded by sea to Cartagena for the reconquest of Nueva Granada, with 8500 troops. Of these, 5000 were Spaniards and the rest Venezuelans, under the command of General Francisco Tomás Morales.*

While Bolívar was at the Island of Jamaica, Morillo's powerful army, aided by the local remnants of the Spanish

---

* Morales became Commander in Chief of the Boves troops after the latter was killed at the battle of Urica on December 5, 1814.

colonials, succeeded in not only taking Cartagena but in re-establishing the Spanish Viceroyalty of Santa Fé, after recon-quering Nueva Granada.

During his exile in Jamaica the Liberator was not idle. Perhaps one of the greatest masterpieces of his pen, which so admirably depicts his profound insight on politics and government, is the so-called "Jamaica Letter" addressed by him to a gentleman of the island, on September 6, 1815, in which he analyzed the causes of the American failure and his reasons for his faith in the final success of liberating his country. Referring to the Spanish colonies in America, he said:

"The colonies represent on a military map an area of 2000 longitudinal and 900 latitudinal leagues (one league: about 3 miles) at its greatest point, wherein 16,000,000 Americans either defend their rights or suffer repression at the hands of Spain, which, although once the world's greatest empire, is now too weak, with what little is left her, to rule the new hemisphere or even to maintain herself in the old. And shall Europe, the civilized, the merchant, the lover of liberty, allow an aged serpent, bent only on satisfying its venomous rage, to devour the fairest part of our globe? What! Is Europe deaf to the clamor of her own interests? Has she no eyes to see justice? Has she grown so hardened as to become insensible? The more I ponder these questions, the more I am confused. I am led to think that America's disappearance is desired; but this is impossible, because all Europe is not Spain. What madness for our enemy to hope to reconquer America when she has no Navy, no funds, and almost no soldiers! Those troops which she has are scarcely adequate to keep her own people in a state of forced obedience and to defend herself from her neighbors. On the other hand, can that nation carry on the exclusive commerce of one-half of the world when it lacks manufactures, agricultural products, crafts and sciences, and even a policy? Assume that this mad venture were successful, and further assume that pacification ensued, would not the sons of the Americans today, together with the sons of the European RECONQUISTADORES twenty years hence, conceive the same patriot designs that are now being fought for?"

And further on, referring to the inefficacy of the Democratic and Federal System for the new-born States, he says:

"As long as our countrymen do not acquire the abilities and political virtues that distinguish our brothers of the north, wholly popular systems far from working to our advantage will, I greatly fear, bring about our downfall. . . . We are dominated by the vices that one learns under the rule of a nation like Spain, which has distinguished itself only in ferocity, ambition, vindictiveness and greed."

Then, with great political perception, he looks into the future and in his imagination conceives a Confederation of States in the New World (The Pan American Union came into being as a result of his foresight) and says:

"It is a grandiose idea to think of consolidating the New World into a single nation, united by pacts into a single bond. It is reasoned that, as these parts have a common origin, language, customs, and religion, they ought to have a single government to permit the newly formed States to unite into a Confederation. But this is not possible. Actually, America is separated by climatic differences, geographic diversity, conflicting interests, and dissimilar characteristics. How beautiful it would be if the Isthmus of Panama could

37

be for us what the Isthmus of Corinth was for the Greeks! Would to God that some day we may have the good fortune to convene there an august assembly of representatives of republics, kingdoms, and empires to deliberate upon the high interests of peace and war with the nations of the other three quarters of the globe. . . ."

And referring to Central America, he says:

"The States of the Isthmus of Panama, as far as Guatemala, will perhaps form a Confederation. Because of their magnificent position between two mighty oceans, they may in time become the emporium of the world. Their canals will shorten distances throughout the world, strengthen commercial ties between Europe, America and Asia, and bring to that happy area tribute from the four quarters of the globe. There, some day perhaps, the capital of the world may be located—reminiscent of Emperor Constantine's claim that Byzantium was the capital of the ancient world."

As to his own country, he said: "New Granada will unite with Venezuela if they can agree to the establishment of a Central Republic. . . ."

This latter dream of his imagination he was able to convert into a reality scarcely four years later.

The Liberator ends his letter with the following paragraph:

"I shall tell you with what we must provide ourselves in order to expel the Spaniards and to found a free government. It is UNION, obviously; but such union will come about through sensible planning and well-directed actions rather than by divine magic. America stands together because it is abandoned by all other nations. It is isolated in the center of the world. It has no diplomatic relations, nor does it receive any military assistance; instead, America is attacked by Spain which has more military supplies than we can possibly acquire through furtive means.

"When success is not assured, when the State is weak and when results are distantly seen, all men hesitate; opinion is divided, passions rage, and the enemy fans these passions in order to win an easy victory because of them. As soon as we are strong and under the guidance of a liberal nation which will lend us her protection, we will achieve accord in cultivating the virtues and talents that lead to glory. Then we will march majestically toward the great prosperity for which South America is destined. Then will those sciences and arts which, born in the East, have enlightened Europe, wing their way to a free Colombia, which will cordially bid them welcome."

It was while at Kingston, that an attempt was made to assassinate the Liberator. Among the many military and civilian patriots that had emigrated from Venezuela to the Island and came to the Liberator for financial assistance, was a man by the name of Amestoy. As Bolívar was destitute of cash, he offered Amestoy to share his lodgings with him. Bolívar used to sleep in a hammock while Amestoy used the only bed in the room. It is narrated that the then Captain General of Venezuela, Moxó, who had put a price on Bolívar's head, commissioned a Spaniard living in Jamaica to have the Liberator eliminated. The Spaniard paid a negro slave to do the job. One night Amestoy arrived early, and as it was a rather hot evening he went to sleep in the hammock, while Bolívar coming in later, and finding his hammock occupied, took to the bed. An hour or so later, the slave armed with a knife, killed Amestoy in the hammock thinking it was Bolívar. The negro was apprehended and condemned to hang.

From Jamaica, Bolívar went to Haiti, where he succeeded in organizing a small expedition (consisting of 250 troops and a few sail ships). He set out for Venezuela on March 30, 1816. His Chief of Staff was General Santiago Mariño, and his deputy was Ducoudray Holstein, a Frenchman who had fought at Waterloo under Napoleon and who was later replaced by Colonel Carlos Soublette.*

Luís Brion, a Curacao sailor-merchant who owned some of the schooners of the expedition, was given the pompous title of Admiral. Upon Bolívar's arrival at Margarita he issued the following proclamation on May 8, 1816:

> "Venezuelans: I have not come to give you laws; but I beg of you to hear my voice. . . . Spaniards living in Venezuela: The war to the death will cease if you stop it! Otherwise, we will take just reprisals and you will be exterminated. Venezuelans: Do not be afraid of the sword of your Liberators; you are always innocent to your brothers!"

One month later Bolívar landed with his small group of soldiers in Tierra Firme (The Port of *Carúpano*) and on July 6, 1816 at the Port of Ocumare, nearly fifty years before Lincoln issued the Emancipation Proclamation, Bolívar issued a decree giving freedom to the slaves who joined his army and offering to compensate their owners. He said in part:

* Soublette: Born in Caracas 1788, died in Caracas February 11, 1870. Was aide-de-camp to Miranda in 1811 and 1812. In 1813 was military secretary to Ribas. Was at Margarita until the arrival of Morillo; defended Cartagena against that Spanish General, and then left for Haiti to join Bolívar. Soublette was President of Venezuela in 1837 and 1838.

"That unfortunate segment of our brothers that has suffered the miseries of slavery is already free. Nature, Justice and Politics demand the emancipation of slavery. From now on there will be in Venezuela only one class: All will be citizens!"

Unfortunately, Bolívar's army was small and soon his scanty contingents were defeated by Morales and compelled to retreat to Güiria, where Generals Mariño and Bermúdez* had proclaimed themselves, in the absence of Bolívar, Supreme Commander and Deputy Supreme Commander of the remnants of the Republican Army and refused to recognize Bolívar's authority. Bolívar was compelled to go into exile for the third time, leaving for Port-au-Prince, Haiti.

While he was at Haiti, Bolívar received Commissioners sent to him by General Arismendi** from Margarita and by the armies of the Center of the country, urging him to return. Zea, one of the Commissioners, and afterward Vice President of the Republic, said to him: "there are still alive a great number of good patriots in Venezuela. The fatherland lives nourishing a hope, but it lacks a superior man capable of transforming that hope into reality. Full of this idea, the people and the army have turned their eyes to General Bolívar as the Supreme Head of the War—the only man who can save them!"

* General José Francisco Bermúdez, born in the Province of Cumaná, January 23, 1782; assassinated December 15, 1831. In June 1819 Bolívar appointed him Supreme Commander of Eastern Venezuela, replacing Mariño. In 1828 the Liberator appointed him Counselor of State.

** Juan Bautista Arismendi, born at Asunción, Capital of Margarita Island, in 1770. Military Governor of Caracas 1814. Took refuge at Margarita after the fall of the Second Venezuelan Republic. In 1817 and 1818 fought in Guayana under Bolívar but was never truly loyal to him. In 1828 he convoked the Caracas Junta which on November 23rd and 26th declared Venezuela separated from Nueva Granada.

Bolívar, with great magnanimity, forgot the insults and outrages he had suffered and agreed to return, this time never to leave the country again. Upon his arrival at Margarita, for the second time, he issued on December 28, 1816, the following proclamation:

"Venezuelans: The people, the Generals and the army, through the medium of General Arismendi have asked me to return. Here I am. I come at the head of a fourth expedition with the brave Admiral Brion to serve you, not to command you!"

As mentioned in a previous chapter, Bolívar's sterling qualities of leadership were greater in adversity than in success. This is perhaps why the most interesting chapter of his life was the one comprising the five-year period between the middle of 1814 and 1819. These were possibly the blackest and most trying years in the history of the Venezuelan Revolution, when Bolívar and his generals suffered a series of disastrous defeats, forcing him to go twice into exile, while his unfortunate country was submerged in a bath of blood and untold sufferings. Much to our regret, our limited space compels us to condense this interesting period into a few paragraphs. However, to understand properly his gigantic task in trying to liberate his country and the manifold obstacles with which he had to contend, we will briefly describe them here.

Venezuela, with a territory one and one third larger than the State of Texas, before the revolution had a scanty population of only 900,000 inhabitants. The bloody reprisals of the Spaniards during the revolution reduced this number to perhaps 600,000. This vast expanse of land, thus scarcely populated, had enormous desert regions and was lacking in adequate roads and bridges, outside the coastal central district. To make the task of the Liberator almost superhuman, the native population, except for a few upper class groups, was for the most part ignorant and prejudiced against any change in their primitive colonial system of government, to which they had been accustomed for the previous 300 years. Furthermore, in his military operations, Bolívar had to contend with his group of young Generals. Although in the majority they were brilliant young men, genuinely loyal to him, there were a few like Generals Mariño, Bermúdez, Páez and Piar, who were overly ambitious and who, while acknowledging his leadership in times of misfortune, were prone after a military victory to rebel and act independently of his authority. The conciliatory nature of the Liberator, however, brought these officers time and again into his fold by overlooking their attempts at insubordination. Nevertheless, these internal dissensions and jealousies on the part of some of his staff were responsible for weakening the strength and unity of the patriots and unduly prolonged the fight for independence.

Another adverse factor of Bolívar's tasks was the pitiful lack of resources of the country, as a result of the protracted war. While the Spaniards were being continuously supplied with soldiers, arms and ammunition by the Mother Country, and obtained food and provided for their other local needs by resorting to plunder and terrorization of the hapless Venezuelan towns, Bolívar, who was absolutely destitute of everything, could not, and in his role of Liberator was repugnant to, exact further sufferings and sacrifices from his countrymen in order to supply his armies.

From Margarita, Bolívar proceeded to Barcelona on the mainland, after Generals Mariño and Bermúdez, repenting their insurrection at Güiria, had acknowledged his authority. Leaving his small detachment of troops in Barcelona, he decided to go to Guayana with an entourage of only fifteen officers and a few attendants, to join with the forces of General

Piar, who, although he too had formerly rebelled against Bolívar's authority, now welcomed the opportunity to serve under him. He chose Guayana because of its strategic position. Its territory, with an area of about one-third the size of the entire country, had as its capital the City of Angostura (now Ciudad Bolívar) strategically situated on the right bank of the Orinoco River. In a letter to Marquis del Toro at Jamaica, Bolívar, referring to Guayana, said:

"This province is a capital point, excellent to be defended and better for taking the offensive. We are at the back of the enemy from here to Santa Fé, and we possess an immense territory on both sides of the Orinoco, Apure, Meta and Arauca Rivers. Besides we possess cattle and horses, and as at present the fighting is confined to holding the ground we have and to prolonging the campaign, the side that obtains these advantages will be the victor."

It was at Quiamare, in the most intricate part of the jungle bordering the Orinoco river valley, that an attempt was made on Bolívar's life. It is related that a mulatto Jesús Alemán, at the head of a platoon of enemy troops was waiting for the Liberator, to assassinate him and his companions.

But Colonel Parejo, who was reconnoitering the jungle, ahead of Bolívar's group, discovered the ambush of the enemy and alerted the others, who instantly dismounted, and feigning to be waiting the arrival of a numerous force that they had left behind, gave orders in a loud voice to attack the flanks and center where the enemy was located; and as a result of these shouts, some shots were heard coming from the rear. Alemán and his guerrillas fled in a panic.

While on his way to Angostura, at the Casacoima Canal, on the Orinoco River, the Spanish river fleet defeated the small boats of the patriots, which made it necessary for the Liberator to spend the night hidden in a nearby swamp, in order to escape being ambushed. Undeterred, he addressed the small group of his followers and with the greatest enthusiasm told them of his plans for his future campaigns that would liberate Santa Fé (Bogotá) and Quito, after which he would carry on to Perú, the Land of the Sun, and up to Potosí, his banners of redemption.

Such ideas, representing the clear picture of the august mission with which Bolívar believed himself entrusted, were looked upon at the time and place as dreams of an unbalanced imagination and appeared so extravagant that Captain Martel, (Larrazábal, the historian, narrates this anecdote) when he heard them expressed, told one of his officers: "Now we are truly lost—The Liberator has gone insane.

Upon arrival at Angostura, Bolívar, with his unmatched generalship and his restless activity, lost no time in organizing a provisional government and from the scattered groups fighting individually in the interior he built up a regular army under his supreme central command. To bring discipline into his forces, Bolívar was compelled to court-martial and have shot one of his most brilliant officers, General Manuel Piar, who three years before, when the Liberator was defeated, had refused to recognize his authority and had encouraged the troops to rebel against Bolívar.

When the Liberator returned from exile, Piar, who had regained his favor with two brilliant victories over the Spaniards, was placed in command of an important post. Here again, however, he began to sow the seeds of discord against the Supreme Chief and against his government. As Piar was a mulatto,* he tried to gain the allegiance of his troops by

* Piar's complexion was almost white. His father was born in the Canary Islands, and his mother was a mulatto from Curaçao.

favoring the half-castes and mestizos over the whites, and lost no opportunity to foment racial discord among his officers and men. Furthermore, he attempted to spread discontent and insubordination among the other military encampments. Bolívar tried to reason with him, and when he found it was to no avail, had him taken prisoner and tried before a court-martial composed of officers and friends of Piar. On October 15, 1817, Piar was condemned to be shot for the crimes of insubordination, desertion, sedition and conspiracy. The sentence was carried out the following day.

One of the most trying periods for the Liberator was the year 1818. The Republic appeared to be agonizing. The Spaniards were masters of all of the center and west of the country. In the eastern Provinces, in addition to the menace of the Spaniards, the lack of unity among the patriot generals continued to exist. Generals Mariño, Arismendi and Páez, each operating independently of Bolívar, at times victorious but more often defeated, were difficult to bring back into the fold of the Central Government.

It was in this fateful year, that a third attempt was made to assassinate the Liberator. He was encamped with a small contingent of troops at a place called "El Rincón de los Toros," located about 130/150 miles southwest of Caracas; while the enemy was intrenched a few miles away, under Spanish Colonel Rafael López. Taking advantage that a defected Sergeant had furnished him with the password of the patriot's camp, López sent a platoon of 8 selected soldiers under Captain Mariano Renovales to assassinate Bolívar.

Meeting suddenly in the darkness of the early hours of the morning with Colonel Santander, Chief of Staff of Bolívar, Renovales gave him the password, and said he was looking for the Liberator to render to him personally an account of his reconnoitering mission of the enemy's position. Santander guided Renovales and his group to a clump of trees, and pointed, among a cluster of hammocks, to a white one where Bolívar was supposed to be sleeping. Whereupon the conspirators immediately discharged their rifles in that direction, killing several of the officers sleeping there. However, Bolívar miraculously escaped being hit by the bullets, because a few moments before he had left his hammock to look for his horse.

In spite of this chain of misfortunes and distressing events, the singleness of purpose of the Liberator was unshaken. His ideal of liberty and hegemony of South America was fixed in his mind. Thus, in the midst of these calamities, he wrote Don Juan Martín Pueyrredon, Supreme Director of the Provinces of the Río de la Plata, at Buenos Aires, on June 12, 1818:

"Most Excellent Sir,

When the triumph of Venezuela's arms has completed the work of independence, or when more favorable circumstances permit us more frequent communication and closer relations, we for our part, will hasten with lively interest to establish the American pact; which, in forming a body politic comprising all our Republics shall present America to the world in an aspect of majesty and grandeur, greater than any that history has recorded. An America thus united —should Heaven grant us that devout wish—could truly style herself the Queen of Nations and the Mother of Republics.

"I hope that the Río de la Plata, with her powerful influence, will cooperate actively in perfecting the political edifice which we initiated on the first day of our struggle for freedom."

It was at this time, when adversity was most trying, that he conceived a vast plan of action which under such sad cir-

cumstances seemed plain insanity. To convoke a National
Congress, to establish a Constitutional Government . . . and
to cross the Andes, liberate Nueva Granada, to create Colombia, giving at the same time the coup de grâce to all Spanish
domination in South America—everything in this dream was
soon to be realized.

His proclamation of October 22, 1818, convoking the National Congress ended with the following sentence:

"Our soldiers have fought to save their brothers, wives,
fathers and sons; not to place them in chains. The Venezuelan army only imposes upon you the condition that you
preserve intact the sacred gift of liberty. I impose upon you
another, as just and necessary, for the fulfillment of this
precious condition: That you elect as your representatives
the most virtuous of your fellow citizens, and forget if you
can in your elections those who have liberated you. On my
part, I renounce forever the authority you have conferred
upon me and would never accept any other than simply the
military one, and that only while this horrendous war continues in Venezuela. The first day of peace will be the last
of my command."

At the inauguration of the Congress on February 15, 1819
Bolívar delivered an address which, together with his Jamaica
letter, may be considered as perhaps the foremost expression
of his superb political creed.* He ended as follows:

"I pray you, Legislators, grant to Venezuela a government
preëminently popular, preëminently just, preëminently
moral; one that will suppress anarchy, oppression, and guilt

* For the sake of brevity we are prevented from publishing here the
text of this remarkable address of the Liberator.

—a government that will usher in the reign of innocence, humanity and peace; a government wherein the rule of inexorable law will signify the triumph of equality and freedom.

"Gentlemen: you may begin your labors—I have finished mine!"

CHAPTER VI

Liberation of Nueva Granada

O N August 26, 1818, five months before the installation of the Congress, Bolívar in preparation for his forthcoming campaign to liberate Nueva Granada had sent Brigadier General Francisco de Paula Santander* with other officers to the Province of Casanare to organize the various small groups of soldiers scattered in that vast province into a Division to help in his plan of invading Nueva Granada.

Santander carried with him a Proclamation from Bolívar to the Granadinos, dated in Angostura August 15, 1818, which ended:

> "The blood of more than 20,000 Spaniards has drenched the soil of Venezuela. Hundreds of glorious battles fought by the armies of liberation have proved to Spain that the avengers of America are as just as its defenders are noble. . . . The Spanish Empire has pitted its enormous resources against handfuls of men who, though unarmed and barely clothed, were inspired by freedom. . . . Generous war-hardened foreigners have come to place themselves under the standards of Venezuela." **

And he continued:

* See page 57 of this chapter about Santander.
** Bolívar here refers to the British Legionnaires who began arriving in Angostura in 1818 to serve under his banners. It was with the aid of these foreign soldiers, who, together with the armies of Bermúdez and Mariño and the plainsmen of Páez, united and directed by the genius of Bolívar, that final victory was achieved.

"Granadinos! America's day has come; no human power can stop the course of nature guided by the hand of Providence. Join your efforts to those of your brothers. . . . Already our advance-guard fills whole provinces of your territory with the luster of its arms; and that same advance-guard, powerfully aided, will hurl the destroyers of Nueva Granada into the seas. The sun will not have completed the course of its present round without beholding in all your territory the proud shrines of liberty!"

This prophecy was soon to be realized— The battle of Boyacá that liberated Nueva Granada took place on August 7, 1819.

While these events were taking place, Spain was trying at the Congress of Aquistrán, convoked at the request of Ferdinand VII, to secure the good offices of the high European powers to bring back into the fold of the Mother Country the South American Colonies which had declared their independence. This gave the Liberator a rare opportunity to issue a declaration in the name of the Republic of Venezuela on November 20, 1818, which ended as follows:

"1.—That the Republic of Venezuela by divine and human rights has been emancipated from the Spanish Nation and has been constituted into an independent, sovereign free state.

   2.—That Spain has no just grounds (justification) to claim its domination and neither has Europe any right to try to subjugate it to the Spanish Government.

   3.—That Venezuela has not requested and will not request its incorporation to the Spanish Nation.

   4.—That Venezuela has not solicited the mediation of the high powers for reconciliation with Spain.

5.—That Venezuela will never deal with Spain except as an equal, either at peace or at war, as all nations reciprocally do.

6.—That Venezuela wishes the mediation of the high powers only to exert their good offices in favor of humanity, inviting Spain to adjust and conclude a treaty of peace and friendship with the Venezuelan Nation."

The seventh paragraph ended: . . . "and the people of Venezuela are determined to bury themselves whole within its ruins if Spain, Europe and the World insist in chaining it to the Spanish yoke."

This declaration of Bolívar which, under the pitiful circumstances prevailing at Angostura, seemed rather a hollow boast, was responsible nevertheless for the creation of confidence at home by bolstering the national pride and was construed abroad as a manifestation of strength by those who were unaware of the true condition of the patriots.

The Congress convoked by Bolívar on February 15, 1819 consisted of 29 Deputies (out of 35, or 5 representatives per Province) representing the Provinces of Caracas, Barcelona, Cumaná, Barinas, Guayana, Margarita and Casanare. This last province belonged to Nueva Granada but the Venezuelan patriots were in occupation. After the installation of the Congress, Bolívar divested himself of civil authority and also resigned his commission in the army. Congress, as expected, confirmed Bolívar in his command and in addition appointed him President of the Republic and Francisco Antonio Zea as Vice President.

A month later, with a group of soldiers of the British contingent, Bolívar left Angostura and on March 11, 1819 joined with the Anzoátegui's Infantry Division stationed at the confluence of the Arauca and the Orinoco Rivers. The soldiers' food in this region, and that in Apure Plains, consisted of only a chunk of roasted beef of inferior quality, weighing about two pounds. Salt and bread were so scarce as to be practically non-existent. Shortly thereafter the small contingents of the Bolívar troops met with the Páez Llanero Division, encamped on the south bank of the mighty Arauca River, some 500 miles south of Caracas. On the other side of the river and stationed about half a mile from its banks, at a point called "Las Queseras del Medio" were 6000 Spanish troops under General Pablo Morillo.

On April 2, 1819 the Liberator sent General Paéz with a group of 150 selected llaneros (cavalry) on a reconnaissance expedition across the river to ascertain the strength and position of the enemy. It was at this place that occurred one of the most memorable hand to hand combats of the wars of independence, comparable only to the Homeric Epic of the Pass of the Thermopylae, fought nearly 2500 years ago. This small group, carrying their crude saddles on their heads and their lances between their teeth, swam against the strong current, guiding their horses at the same time. By a surprise attack on Morillo's army, killing in their onslaught some 500 enemies, the llaneros of Paéz were able to withdraw and recross the river, with the insignificant loss of only eight casualties.

Two days later Morillo, misjudging the strength of the Liberator's army, withdrew his forces to Achaguas, and as the rainy season was about to begin, he crossed the River Apure heading north to his winter headquarters at Calabozo, a town located about halfway between the Apure River and Caracas. He arrived at Calabozo twelve days later.

Meanwhile the small Bolívar army, 3000 strong, began the march on the savannah, parallel to the River Arauca en route to Nueva Granada. At a hamlet, called Guamito, on May 15th, the Liberator received a communication from General Santander, telling of his success in defeating the Spanish bands of soldiers roaming through the plains of Casanare. Casanare is a province of plains, similar to those of Apure, crisscrossed by mighty rivers and bordered on the west by the imposing Colombian Andes, on the other side of which are situated the valleys and high plateaus of Bogotá (Santa Fé). Bolívar immediately recognized the advantages that could be derived if he could successfully invade Nueva Granada through Casanare.

During the rainy season the plains become immense swamps, entirely isolated from the rest of the country. Therefore the enemy, retiring to its winter quarters, would have no means of knowing the whereabouts of the patriot army. As regards the Royalist army garrisoning Nueva Granada, as it was felt that the rains protected them from an invasion from Casanare, their various detachments were scattered in widely separated areas which Bolívar could attack piecemeal, by surprise. Furthermore, the Liberator thought that public opinion should then be favorable to the operations of the patriots, and from all these premises he deduced that although he was undertaking a campaign handicapped by so many difficulties, the results should be favorable to the cause of America.

Bolívar described his plan to General Paéz and obtained his cooperation, and a week later, in a ruined hut in the abandoned village of Setenta, on the Apure River, the Liberator convoked a war council consisting of his principal officers. It was attended by Generals Soublette and Anzoátegui, also by Briceño Méndez, Carrillo, Iribarren, Rangel, Rooke, Plaza and Manrique. As the hut was completely devoid of furnishings, lacking even chairs or benches, all present sat on the skulls of cattle that had been slaughtered to ration the troops. It was at this humble place that the invasion of Nueva Granada was decided and instructions were immediately sent by Bolívar to Vice President Zea at Angostura, to Generals Bermúdez and Mariño, operating in eastern Venezuela, as well as to the other commanders operating in the central and northern part of the country.

There were three routes leading through the Province of Tunja to the high plateau where Santa Fé (Bogotá) was situated:

1.—Route of Labranza Grande
2.—Route of Salina de Chita
3.—Route of Páramo de Pisba

Bolívar rejected the route through Labranza Grande because it led directly to Mongua, near Sogamoso, on the other side of the Andes, where a strong contingent of Spanish troops had its winter headquarters. Instead, the Liberator favored the route through the Salina de Chita, and so told his Generals, because it was the shortest and there were a few small villages on this trail, which could provide suitable shelter for the troops. However, because most of the traffic from the plains moved through this route, he knew it was strongly garrisoned by the Spaniards at various strategic points, where his small army could easily be destroyed. Without divulging his plan, Bolívar finally decided to choose the route through the Páramo de Pisba even though it crossed the most formidable and perilous region of the mountains, through an almost nonexistent trail. This route had the advantage over the other two of placing his army at the rear guard of the enemy, where he was least expected. It was only a few days after the troops were again on the march that Bolívar let his officers in on the secret of his new plan of attack.

Exclusive of the troops under General Páez, which remained in the llanos, the small Bolívar army consisted of only four

battalions and together with the British legion detachment
totaled about   1300 men
   Plus the artillery consisting of four small
cannons under Colonel Salom, with a contingent of   40 men
And seven cavalry squadrons totaling   870 men
_____
2210 men

Besides there was the man-power handling the impedimenta, baggage, and cattle on the hoof. This army was soon to be increased by about 1200 additional troops under General Santander, stationed at Tame in the foothills of the Andes, some 350 miles away; or a grand total fighting force of about 3400 men. The Spanish army of Nueva Granada, garrisoned in the provinces about to be invaded by Bolívar was estimated at about 7000 strong, but it was scattered and subdivided into small contingents over a wide area.

It took Bolívar's army one month to cover the distance between the Apure River and the Village of Tame. Under torrential tropical rains, and with no roads or bridges, they had to cross the swollen rivers in makeshift canoes. The toll in casualties in the ranks, caused by disease, desertions and other calamities due to the inclement weather was appalling. Only 1850 men arrived in Tame to join the Santander division. Altogether, about 3000 troops left Tame on their way to conquer Nueva Granada.

But if the loss in men was great, it was worse in the number of animals. Half of the horses and cattle perished. Only the guiding genius and superb leadership of the Liberator kept the troops on the march against these hardships. Bolívar, who was not yet thirtysix, had at the time perfect health, amazing morale and physical endurance. He never complained of fatigue after a strenuous journey, during which he often helped to load the mule trains as well as to unload the canoes serving as transports to ford the rivers. He never rejected the most humble or menial task in helping his soldiers. His army was integrated by young men, impervious to weather, fatigue or the hazards of their difficult undertaking.

The three top officers under Bolivar were:

General Carlos Soublette:—29 years old, second in rank, as Chief of Staff. (See footnote about Soublette on Page 40, Chapter V.)

General Francisco de Paula Santander:—Born in Cúcuta in 1792; died at Santa Fé (Bogotá) on May 6, 1840; Vice President of Colombia from 1821 to 1828; implicated in the conspiracy against Bolívar; was imprisoned at Cartagena; resumed public life in 1831 and was elected President of Colombia 1832, 1839.

General José Antonio Anzoátegui:—Born in 1789. Commander of the Rear Guard Division. He had an irascible temper, was always ill-humored, full of complaints, and found fault with everything. But he was a great disciplinarian, and his generalship and daring in leading his troops into combat were unmatched. Scarcely two months later he was to wring a splendid victory at Boyacá, the battle which sealed the independence of Nueva Granada. Anzoátegui died at Pamplona, three months after Boyacá, on November 15, 1819, while on his way to liberate Maracaibo. He was thirty years old.

Under Anzoátegui was Colonel James Rooke, who commanded the British legion. Rooke was exactly the opposite of Anzoátegui. He was always content with everything and with life as he found it. For Rooke the Apure climate was mild and healthy and superior to any other until he encountered that of the high plateaus of Nueva Granada, which to him had no rival in the world. To Rooke, his soldiers were the best in the world, and if one of them died he consoled himself with the thought that he had deserved to die. When at the hamlet of Pore, the Liberator observed that Rooke was wearing a mili-

57

tary tunic that was in shreds and he had no shirt. Bolívar asked his orderly to supply one of his own shirts to Rooke. To which the orderly is said to have remarked: "Which one? Your Excellency has only two shirts—the one you are wearing and the other, in shreds, is being laundered."

After the crossing of the Andes, Rooke joined the main contingents of the army with his battalion at the village of Bonza. Upon calling on Bolívar he found the Liberator seated on a small piece of luggage, with his lunch before him, consisting of roasted beef, bread and chocolate placed on a small wooden bench. Bolívar asked Rooke how his men had fared crossing the Andes. Rooke, as usual replied they had fared very well and were in excellent shape. At the invitation of Bolívar he joined him in his frugal lunch, saying he had never tasted better food in his life. At this juncture, General Anzoátegui arrived, in bad humor. "What is the news?" asked the Liberator. Anzoátegui replied: "Do you know the condition of the British legion commanded by Rooke?" The Liberator said, "Certainly, the Colonel has just given me the most favorable information, saying he had not suffered any losses in the Páramo (bleak plains)." Anzoátegui then proceeded to inform Bolívar that one-fourth of the British soldiers plus two officers had perished during the crossing. To which Rooke replied: "I don't deny it, but it is also true that those men were the worst soldiers in my brigade, and it has gained with their death." Rooke died three days later, after the battle of Pantano de Vargas, from a wound sustained while charging like a lion at the head of his battalion.

The last fifty miles of plains before reaching the foothills of the Andes, when they arrived at Pore, were to be the most trying. The tropical rains, worse than any monsoon in India, had transformed the region into a small inland sea and the troops were compelled to march waist-deep in water. At Pore, obstacles of a different nature were encountered. The gigantic Andes, considered impassable in the rainy season, appeared as an impregnable barrier in the path of Bolívar's army.

The llaneros (plainsmen) accustomed to the torrid climate of the tropics and entirely destitute of clothing, were terrified at the stupendous heights and amazed that a country so different to theirs existed. Men accustomed to tame wild horses, to overpowering, single-handed, savage bulls of the plains, and to dealing, without fear, with tigers and alligators, were frightened at the forbidding sight of the Andes. And if the frigid air of the mountains did not kill them, the cold water from the melting snows, to which the soldiers were unaccustomed, produced a wholesale epidemic of diarrhea. In writing from the small settlement of Paya to Vice President Zea at Angostura, the Liberator said:

"The abruptness of the mountains is incredible. In four marches all of the horses and mules transporting the ammunition have perished, and we have lost all the replacements of the cattle."

At Paya he took time to issue a proclamation to the Granadinos which ended:

"Do not be afraid of those who come to shed their blood to make Colombia a free and independent nation. The Granadinos are innocent before the eyes of the Liberating Army, of the Congress, and of the President of the Republic. For us the only guilty ones are the Spanish tyrants, and even then they will perish only on the field of battle."

Bolívar took special care to have this Proclamation distributed throughout the high valleys surrounding Bogotá and Tunja, where it produced the double effect of arousing in its inhabitants the sentiment of the injustices suffered and their desire to avenge them.

It took the army two weeks to reach the end of the climb—the top of the pass, 13,000 feet high, the dreaded Páramo de Pisba; a bleak, cruel, mountain plateau, swept by piercing winds. The worst was over. A few days more of easy descent and the troops straggled into the high valleys of the Sogamoso, bright with sun and green with vegetables.

Bolívar had crossed the Andes. Of the 3000 men who had begun the ascent on the other side, only 1600 scarecrows wandered into the village of Socha, around July 6, 1819. When the soldiers saw behind them the high peaks of the mountains covered with forbidding clouds and fog, they made the spontaneous vow of fighting to conquer or dying at the hands of the enemy rather than to withdraw to Venezuela through the same route. They feared the Andes more than they feared the enemy, no matter how formidable the latter.

General Mangin, the French hero of the First World War, while visiting Perú in 1924, on the occasion of the centennial of the battle of Ayacucho, described Bolívar's crossing of the Peruvian Andes as "the most magnificent episode in the history of war." However, Bolívar's army in the campaign that liberated Perú had crossed the Cordillera Blanca (White Cordillera), a much higher range of mountains than those of Nueva Granada, without sustaining any losses because the Liberator for several months had been preparing for this crossing by furnishing his troops with proper equipment of double clothing, shoes, overcoats and blankets. Furthermore the men had been well-trained in advance to endure the high altitudes. The soldiers camped for the night in good shelters, well-provided with food and cordwood, and the horses were properly shod and supplied with blankets for the cold weather. During the crossing of the Colombian Andes, Bolívar was destitute of everything; his army was in tatters and the horses and mules, unshod, had to climb the precarious abandoned mountain trails. This resulted in tragic losses in men and animals.

The Spaniards could not understand how the cordilleras had been crossed. The inhabitants of the high Colombian plateaus, weary of the enemy's depredations and of the yoke of centuries, brought munitions, food, horses and clothing to the Venezuelans, and hundreds of peasants joined the liberating army. After such privations, nothing more was needed to put Bolívar's men in good heart.

The master stroke of the genius of Bolívar in invading the country through its back door paid invaluable dividends to him in the victories that followed. From the start, his bold maneuver gave him a twofold advantage: The enemy did not expect an invasion in the midst of the tropical torrential rainy season; and the invaded valleys were completely unprepared to be defended properly.

With his superhuman energy and unshaken perseverance the Liberator in the short period of four weeks increased his depleted army to 3000 men, properly equipped and well-fed. He succeeded besides in engaging in a series of piecemeal combats the enemy garrisons scattered in various detachments in the region. This culminated in the battle of "Pantano de Vargas" on July 25, 1819. Here the tired battalions of the patriots, not yet fully recovered from their recent exhaustive ordeal, succeeded in defeating the Spaniards under General Barreiro, but only after Bolívar, seeing his troops giving way to the ferocious Spanish onslaught, sent a squadron of llaneros under Colonel Rondón into the affray, with these words: "Colonel, save the Fatherland!" Rondón, with his llaneros, and Rooke with his British legionnaires, soon turned the tide of the battle in favor of the patriots. The Spaniards suffered

500 casualties plus the loss of part of their arms and ammunition, while the patriots had in dead and wounded 104 men and officers. Among the latter was Colonel Rooke of the British Legion.

General Manuel Antonio López, who at that time was a lieutenant, narrates in his memoirs that Rooke, while brilliantly attacking at the head of his battalion, suffered a wound in his left arm, which splintered the bones at the elbow, necessitating its amputation. He died of gangrene three days later. Bolívar decorated the victors with the Cross of the Liberator, particularly the British Battalion, for their gallantry.

Bolívar, after this victory, through a series of strategic movements, and in a stroke of audacity, on August 5th occupied the City of Tunja, virtually placing himself and his troops at the back of Barreiro's army, and cutting off the line of communications of the Spaniards with Bogotá. In Tunja he found a copious booty of arms, food, medicines and urgently needed clothing for his troops. When Barreiro became aware that his rival was at Tunja, to escape the trap he hastily moved his army at night in a circuitous route, in an endeavor to reach the bridge over the Boyacá River, about ten miles from Tunja, where the main road to Bogotá, about 100 miles distant, was located. On the morning of August 7th, Bolívar, who had his troops at the ready, in the main square of Tunja, upon hearing of Barreiro's march, ordered his army to pursue, with instructions to intercept the enemy at any cost and force him into battle. At two o'clock in the afternoon the two armies faced each other about three-quarters of a mile from the Boyacá River bridge.

While the patriots had 3000 men—the same number as the Spaniards—only 2000 were veterans; the rest were green recruits, with scarcely any training. In spite of this inferiority in numbers and skill, Bolívar succeeded by his superb strategy in cutting Barreiro's army in two, and then proceeded piecemeal to destroy first its left flank, then its center and finally its right, deployed on the other side of the Boyacá bridge. It was an overwhelming victory for the patriots. Captured with Barreiro and all of his staff were 1600 soldiers, plus all of their arms and ammunition. The Spaniards suffered 210 casualties, among them some of their best officers, while the casualties of the patriots were about half that number. When Bolívar detected among the prisoners the traitor Fernández Vinoni, who seven years previously was responsible for the loss of the Puerto Cabello Forts by delivering them to the enemy, he had him hanged from a tree on the spot.

Following this victory, Bolívar headed for Bogotá with a squadron of llaneros, but receiving news on the way that the Viceroy had fled, he hurried and entered the city with an escort of only a few officers and soldiers, on the afternoon of the 10th. The Viceroy had fled the day before toward Cartagena, with the principal members of his government and a detachment of 200 soldiers. Bogotá gave the Liberator a tumultuous reception. The acclamations of the people, exploding overwhelmingly with joy, could be compared only to their surprise at the sudden and unexpected transition from the most oppressive tyranny to the joy of freedom.

Never was a more complete triumph obtained with so many handicaps and hardships. Seventyfive days after the Council of War at the Apure River, victory had delivered to the Hero the principal Provinces of Nueva Granada. Bolívar remembered at this juncture how four and a half years before he had bade his adieu to the city, and now he was returning as a conqueror, with his fate completely changed. While at Bogotá, Bolívar issued a proclamation on August 24, 1819, which ended as follows:

TO THE SOLDIERS OF THE LIBERATING ARMY:

"Soldiers! You were not 200 in numbers when you started this amazing campaign; now that you are many thousands, all America is too small a theatre for your valor. Yes, soldiers, from the north to the south of this half of the world you will spread the gospel of liberty. Pretty soon the capital of Venezuela will receive you for the third time, and its tyrant will not even dare to wait for us. And wealthy Peru will at the same time be covered with the Standards of Venezuela, Nueva Granada, Argentina and Chile.

"Soldiers! Thousands of glorious battles give you the right to expect other thousands of victories, carrying in your standards as an emblem: BOYACÁ!"

CHAPTER VII

Liberation of Venezuela

BOLÍVAR remained at Bogotá scarcely six weeks, during which short period of time, with his prodigious activity, he organized a provisional government with General Santander as Vice President of Nueva Granada. He reorganized the Treasury, in which he found half a million pesos in silver plus 100,000 pesos in gold bars; cut in half the salaries of the civil and military employees, and set in motion the administrative machinery of the liberated provinces.

At the same time he devoted his attention to the military problems confronting him. He sent General Soublette to occupy the northern Cúcuta valleys. General Manuel Valdés was sent with some troops to the southern provinces, and Lieutenant Colonel Córdova went to Antioquia.

On September 8, 1819 the Liberator issued a proclamation to the Granadians, in which he expressed the same ideas contained in his message to the Angostura Congress regarding uniting Nueva Granada and Venezuela into one Republic. He said in part:

> "My only ambition has been to liberate you from the horrible torture to which you have been subjected by your enemies and to restore to you the full enjoyment of your rights, so that you may freely elect a government of your own and spontaneous choice.
>
> "The reunion of Nueva Granada and Venezuela into one Republic is the innermost desire of all sensible citizens and of the foreigners who love and protect the American cause. I await therefore the sovereign determination of the

Congress to convoke a National Assembly that will decide the incorporation of Nueva Granada! Then you will send your representatives to the General Congress or organize your own Granadine Government.

"I take my departure from you for a short period only. New victories are awaiting the liberating army that will not enjoy any rest while there remain enemies in the north and south of Colombia.

"Meanwhile, you have nothing to fear. I leave with you courageous soldiers for your defense, just magistrates for your protection, and a worthy Vice President to govern you.

"Granadians! Eight of your provinces enjoy liberty. Preserve intact this sacred gift with your virtues, your patriotism and valor. Never forget the ignominy of the outrages you have experienced and you will be free!"

Boyacá had been the crowning achievement of the Liberator. Never in his long and glorious career had he conceived of and inflicted such disastrous military defeat to the enemy as on that epic battlefield. When General Morillo was informed in Venezuela about Boyacá, he wrote the Spanish Minister of War regarding the defeat of Spanish General Barreiro, saying in part:

"The insurrectionist Bolívar has immediately occupied the Capital of Santa Fé, and the fatal success of this battle has placed at his disposal all the kingdom and the immensely wealthy and abundant resources of a very populous country, which will provide him with all that he needs to continue the war of these provinces. The unfortunate defeat at Boyacá delivers to the rebels, besides the new Kingdom of Granada, many ports and harbors in the southern seas, where their pirates will find shelter; Popayan, Quito,

Pasto and all of the interior of this continent up to Perú, where there is not a single soldier, are at the mercy of the one who has possession of Santa Fé, to whom at the same time are open the mints, arsenals, munition plants, factories and everything belonging to the King, our Master in all of the Viceroyalty!"

On September 9, 1819, Bolívar addressed a communication to the fugitive Viceroy Sámano, who was then at Cartegena, proposing an exchange of prisoners. But the vain, aged Viceroy, who thus had the fine opportunity to save the lives of the Boyacá prisoners, did not even answer.

Bolívar left Bogotá on his way to Angostura on September 20, 1819 and three weeks later, on October 11th, General Santander ordered General Barreiro and 38 of his officers executed by a firing squad, in the main square of Bogotá. Santander was greatly criticized both at home and abroad for this action, but he had no alternative. The magnanimous Liberator had provided as a prison for these vanquished Spanish officers commodious quarters, where they were generously treated. Apparently, according to a communication from Santander to Bolívar, dated October 17th, Barreiro and his men, taking advantage of this generosity, tried to spread among their military jailers subversion and insurrection against the Republic, inciting the soldiers to rebellion, and some even tried to escape.

On his triumphal march to the Venezuelan border, the Liberator was overwhelmed with the spontaneous demonstrations in his honor by the joyful peoples of the cities and towns. However, at Chita, on the high pass on the Andes, he received alarming news from Angostura. Bolívar had left Angostura six months before, and during his absence heard rumors that he had failed to liberate Nueva Granada; that his Vice President Zea was deposed and General Arismendi had been appointed in his place, and that General Mariño was reinstated as Chief Commander of the Army of the Eastern Provinces. However, the Liberator's timely return to Angostura on December 11, 1819, which had been preceded by the news of the Boyacá victory, quelled the attempted insurrection. Bolívar acting with great tact and patriotism, appointed the repentant Arismendi as head of the eastern armies in place of Mariño, and with his usual generosity, overlooking the devious designs of his enemies, he was soon able to reestablish peace and concord among the dissident elements in the Congress.

After Boyacá, when Bolívar arrived in Angostura, he addressed a note to Congress, then meeting there, in which he said in part:

"To remedy the precarious situation of friends and relatives that had taken refuge in the Antilles, I took the liberty, while at Bogota in 1819, of borrowing from the Treasury 14,000 Pesos. You have assigned me a salary of 25,000 Pesos a year as Commander in Chief of the Army, plus 50,000 Pesos a year as President of the Republic. I renounce forthwith and forever all of these salaries which I have never received, being completely satisfied with the 14,000 Pesos that I borrowed in Bogota.

"The purpose for which I obtained this loan and the sacred obligations that I fulfilled with this money have more than compensated me for the above rights which I renounce in favor of the public Treasury. This is the expression of my innermost desire. To accept it will be for me a most special grace, that I will consider as the purest testimony with which the National Congress had condescended to honor me."—This splendid donation, the Congress accepted.

To the Congress meeting in special session to hear an account of his military operations, the Liberator mentioned his plan of reuniting the two countries into one Republic, and said in conclusion:

"Legislators! To your wisdom belongs the task of decreeing the great social act and establishing the beginnings of the pact on which this vast Republic is going to be founded. Proclaim it to the face of the world and my services will be rewarded."

After the President of the Congress had replied, Bolívar added:

"Upon your decreeing the political union of both nations, you will have satisfied my innermost desire and overwhelmingly rewarded the army for its services."

Acting accordingly, the fundamental Constitution of the Republic of Colombia was sanctioned at Angostura on December 17, 1819, a date of great significance—when the great Republic was born and also the date on which its founder died eleven years later. The Congress designated as the principal seat of the capital of Colombia the City of Cúcuta, to which city the general government of the Republic was transferred at the beginning of 1821. The Congress elected Bolívar President of Colombia; Zea, Vice President; and Doctor Juan Germán Roscio and General Francisco de Paula Santander Vice Presidents of the Departments of Venezuela and of Cundinamarca respectively.

In the short period of two weeks Bolívar's genius and organizational ability had laid down not only the basis for the foundation of a great Republic but also had dictated the measures necessary to insure its proper functioning. Besides, he tried to establish its credit abroad, for which purpose he sent Vice President Zea on a special mission to London and Manuel Torres on a similar one to the United States. However, Torres never reached his destination—he died while on the way, on one of the Caribbean Islands.

On December 24, 1819 Bolívar left for Bogotá, where he arrived two and a half months later, on March 5, 1820. During his absence from Nueva Granada, General Santander had convoked the authorities and principal inhabitants of Bogotá for the purpose of approving the Union. On this subject the Liberator issued on March 8, 1820 a proclamation in which he said in part:

"Colombians! . . . . . Your fate is going to change. Darkness, fetters, ignorance, misery, will be followed by the sublime gifts of Divine Providence: Freedom, light, honor and happiness.

"Colombians! I promise you in the name of the Congress that you will be regenerated; your institutions will achieve social perfection; your tributes will be abolished; your shackles broken; great virtues will be your inheritance and only talent, valor, and virtue will be rewarded.

"Venezuelans! You have always shown great interest in belonging to the great Republic of Colombia and already your wishes have been fulfilled: the creation of the free, independent Republic of Colombia between two brotherly peoples. I have obtained this. Long live the God of Colombia!"

By coincidence, on the same day King Ferdinand VII surrendered his dictatorial powers and agreed to govern Spain under the Constitution of 1812.

Bolívar's stay in Bogotá was short. Two weeks later, on March 20, 1820, he left for Cúcuta on the northern border of the Republic. At this latter city, where he established the center of his military operations for his forthcoming campaign to liberate Venezuela, he remained five months.

Captain O'Leary, one of his aides-de-camp, gives an interesting account of the sort of life the Liberator led in Cúcuta during this period. We copy the following abstract:

"Bolívar usually awakened at 6:00 A.M., and on leaving his bedroom, which was also his office, he visited the stables to see that his horses were well cared for. After his lunch at 9:00 A.M., he received information from his private secretary, the Secretary of War, and from his Chief of Staff. He listened to these reports, pacing the floor in his office or seated in his hammock, which was also his bed. After his secretary had read to him the various dispatches and memoranda, he dictated his replies at once, concise and to the point. And as he knew personally his officers as well as the principal citizens, and their qualities or defects, he could always solve their petitions on the spot.

"After dispatching the most urgent business, he usually read until 5:00 P.M., when dinner was served. His table as a rule was frugal: soup, roasted or boiled beef or chicken, simply-prepared vegetables, and some sweets. Water was his customary beverage. However, when conditions permitted, better foods and good wine were served to him. Immediately after dinner, which generally lasted an hour, he went horseback riding, accompanied by his secretary. In the evening, he engaged in conversation with his friends or officers who came to visit with him. At 9:00 P.M. he retired to his bedroom and while in his hammock read until 11:00 P.M. His favorite authors were Montesquieu and Rousseau, although he also enjoyed reading history. He had an extraordinary memory for dates, names, and events, and frequently while at dinner he quoted full pages of the author he had been reading, with little variation from the original text. He frequently wrote articles on politics for the Bogota and Angostura newspapers. His style was vigorous and direct, but in his personal correspondence he was stern and at times sarcastic."

While the Liberator was directing the war and the organization of the new army contingents from Cúcuta, he established at that city warehouses for the storage of food and clothing, also for arms, ammunition, in addition to factories for the repair of army equipment and for the manufacture of powder and bullets.

A few days after his arrival in Cúcuta, on the occasion of the Tenth Anniversary of the revolution, on April 19, 1820, he issued a proclamation to the army which ended:

"Soldiers! You have consecrated the most beautiful region of the world to immortality through your glorious victories. On April 19th Colombia was born. Since then you are ten years old."

Aside from his eloquence, the Liberator had very little remuneration to give to the army. A few pesos to the officers and one real (about ten cents) to each soldier was their only compensation. The little money collected by the Treasury was preferentially used for the purchase of arms.

If Bolívar was a great general, he was also a master in the art of politics, knowing how to take advantage of events in the mother country, to capitalize them in favor of his own cause. After the insurrection in Spain that compelled King Ferdinand VII to surrender his dictatorial powers, the Liberator on July 1, 1820 issued the following proclamation to the Spaniards:

"Spaniards! You are the victims of the same persecution as we are; you have been expelled from your homes by the Spanish tyrant, with the horrible alternative of being sacrificed or of becoming executioners of your own brothers. But the day of justice has arrived in your country; the standard of liberty has been unfurled in all the confines of the Peninsula (Iberic Peninsula). There are now free Spaniards. If you prefer the glory of being soldiers of our fatherland to the crime of being the wreckers of America, I offer you in the name of the Republic the most solemn guarantee —Come to us and you will be reintegrated to the bosom of your families, as has already occurred with some of your brothers at arms.

"Liberals! Go and enjoy the blessings of peace and freedom.

"Serfs! Do not be blind any longer; learn to be men."

Preoccupied with the military situation, Bolívar soon left Cúcuta, on August 20, 1920, to activate the operations for the surrender of Cartagena. A month later he was back at the Venezuelan border town of San Cristóbal, where intent on his plan to liberate this country, he decided, as the first step, to reconquer the cities of Mérida and Trujillo. On October 1st he entered the former city and soon thereafter he established his headquarters at Trujillo.

Meanwhile portentous events, favorable to the patriots, were taking place in Spain. After the military uprising against the dictatorial powers of King Ferdinand VII, the newly convoked Spanish Parliament, as one of its first measures, sent instructions to General Morillo to try to win back, through conciliation and friendly negotiations, the Venezuelan and New Granadian insurrectionists. The instructions to Morillo further indicated that, as an inducement to restore the Colonies to the fold of the mother country, he was to promise a number of political concessions, provided they would swear allegiance to the Spánish Constitution of 1812.

As a result of preliminary negotiations between the commissioners of Morillo and those of Bolívar, a six months' armistice was signed at the City of Trujillo, on November 26, 1820, and the following day, at the request of Morillo, who expressed a keen desire to meet the Liberator, an interview was held between the two generals at the neighboring village of Santa Ana. Morillo returned to Spain two weeks later, and was succeeded in the Supreme Command of the Spanish Armies of Tierra Firme (Venezuela and Colombia) by Field Marshall Miguel de la Torre.

In reviewing the events of the year 1820, perhaps the greatest triumph of Colombia, more important than the military, was the political. Public opinion which, before Boyacá, had been adverse to the Patriots was now its principal support. Besides, the territory of the Republic had by this time been expanded with the addition of the Provinces of Mérida and Trujillo as well as part of those of Barinas and Barcelona in Venezuela. In Nueva Granada the Provinces of Santa Marta and Riohacha had been conquered, and in the south, Popayán had been evacuated by the Spaniards. Furthermore, the armies of the patriots had been reinforced by the great number of Americans who had abandoned the Spanish banners.

The beginning of 1821 found the Liberator again at Bogotá. General Manuel Valdés, whom he had previously appointed to command the troops operating in the south of Nueva Granada, had not moved his division toward Pasto with the celerity Bolívar demanded and he was relieved of his command. The

Liberator sent to replace him General Antonio José de Sucre, who at that time was 28 years old. In the next four years, Sucre was to become the Liberator's most highly esteemed officer and the finest of his generals.

Sucre was born in 1793 in Cumaná, served under Miranda, and after the latter capitulated, went into exile at Trinidad. From there he returned to the mainland with General Mariño at the time of the second Republic. He was later incorporated into the general staff of Bolívar, although until 1819 he was practically unknown to the Liberator. While Bolívar was en route to liberate Nueva Granada Sucre was promoted to Brigadier General by Vice President Zea.

It is narrated that when the Liberator, after the battle of Boyacá, was navigating the Orinoco River downstream on the way to Angostura, his boat met up with a smaller one traveling in the opposite direction. Bolívar asked, "Who is traveling on that boat?" He was answered, "General Sucre," to which Bolívar is said to have angrily replied, "There is no such General!" Whereupon he ordered both boats to be moored together. Sucre then explained that although he had been promoted to the rank of General, possibly because his services deserved it, he had never thought of accepting that rank without the prior approval of General Bolívar. The Liberator, instantly understanding the reproach, apologized and from then on the two men who contributed most to the liberation of South America became the closest of friends.

General O'Leary, who at that time was a Captain and an aide-de-camp to the Liberator, narrates that a few months before Sucre had been appointed to command the army of the south, on the day the Liberator arrived in Cúcuta, returning from Cartagena around September 18, 1820, Sucre rode on horseback to the outskirts of the city to meet Bolívar.

75

"Upon seeing Sucre, whom I had never met" narrates O'Leary, "I asked the Liberator, 'Who is that poor rider that is coming toward us?"

"He is," Bolívar replied, "one of the best army officers; he combines the professional military knowledge of Soublette;* the kind nature of Briceño;** the talent of Santander; and the activity of Salom;*** strange as it may seem, he is unknown and his qualities are unsuspected. I am determined to bring him to my side, convinced that soon he will excel me."

Sucre, under Bolívar, liberated Ecuador and Perú, and became the first President of the newly founded Republic of

---

* See page 40, Chapter V.

** Colonel Pedro Briceño Méndez. Minister of War. Born at Barinas of wealthy parents; he was 18 when the revolution started. In 1813 he met Bolívar who appointed him his secretary and after that accompanied the Liberator into exile and defeat and triumph. He refused military rank, but the Liberator finally persuaded him to accept the commission of Colonel in 1818. As Minister of War, his friendly and modest behavior was in great contrast to the irascible and variable character of Bolívar.

*** Colonel Bartolomé Salom, born at Puerto Cabello, August 24, 1780; as Chief of Staff was the direct opposite of Briceño, but the man the Liberator needed by his side. No matter how extravagant Bolívar's orders, Salom never made the slightest protest but faithfully complied with them. O'Leary relates the following anecdote on this: "On one occasion they needed 100 mules to move some troops. Salom received orders to secure them immediately. The government had none in that district and there were none for hire. This was no problem for Salom. He sent scouts out to comb the surrounding country, committing his own personal credit but only when he became convinced that there was not a single mule available within a 100-mile radius, and after substituting for these some other means of transportation, did he inform the Liberator of his inability to comply with his instructions to the letter." Salom never said "NO" or that supplies needed could not be obtained. In 1825 we will see Salom accepting the surrender of the Fortress of Callao in Perú, the last stronghold of the Spanish domination in South América. Salom died in Caracas, October 30, 1863.

Bolívia. He was assassinated in Berruecos on June 4, 1830, six months before Bolívar died.

On April 28, 1821, one month before the expiration of the Armistice, hostilities were resumed by mutual consent, and on that occasion Bolívar issued a proclamation to the army, which ended:

"Soldiers! Place yourselves between the vanquished and your victorious arms, showing that you are as great in generosity as in valor!"

The Armistice had given Bolívar an opportunity to gather his widely dispersed contingents into a great military concentration of men and equipment, capable of inflicting on the enemy a disastrous defeat in a final battle that would destroy the enemy forever. San Carlos was chosen as the focal point of this concentration because of its strategic position as a key center, where the roads converged to the north directly to Valencia and Caracas; to the northwest with Barquisimeto; and to the south with the key cities connecting with the llanos: Guanare and Barinas; also from Guanare branched out the main road to Trujillo and Mérida and the Colombian border. San Carlos was situated equi-distant from Caracas, 170 miles to the north, to Barinas to the south.

The primitive means of transportation of a century and a half ago made it necessary for the infantry to march long distances on foot, while the ammunition and other impedimenta were carried on pack horses and mules. As the main sustenance of the army consisted of beef, requiring the moving of large herds of cattle on the hoof along with the soldiers, any mobilization of a large contingent of men and equipment was a gigantic task.

The army corps under General Páez, operating at the Apure

plains with its headquarters at Achaguas (some 250 miles distant from San Carlos)—totaling about 1000 infantry men, and about 1500 cavalry, was instructed to bring to San Carlos from the plains 2000 spare horses for the cavalry and 4000 head of cattle on the hoof, sufficient to sustain the entire army in the forthcoming campaign. It took the Páez troops one month to reach San Carlos, in the second week of June 1821.

Originally the troops from the various contingents mobilized by Bolívar totaled about 10,000 but, as a result of sickness and desertions, only 6500 troops arrived at San Carlos, which the Liberator distributed into three divisions—the first under General Páez; the second under General Cedeño, and the third under General Plaza. General Mariño, who had joined Bolívar on April 30th, acted as Chief of Staff with General Salom as his assistant.

Thus organized, Bolívar marched his divisions on June 23, 1821 and on the morning of the following day, June 24, 1821, the patriot army reached the heights of Buenavista, about three miles from the plain of Carabobo, twelve miles southwest of Valencia, where Spanish General La Torre was waiting for them with his army, about 6500 strong, or the same number of troops as the patriots. The plain of Carabobo gave La Torre the advantage of covering nearby Puerto Cabello as well as the Pao territory, from where his army was supplied with cattle. From the Buenavista heights Bolívar could observe the enemy ready for battle, assembled in six strong infantry columns and five of cavalry, and situated in such manner as to make it possible for each column mutually to assist the other.

The limited space of this brief biography precludes our describing the battle in detail. Suffice it to mention that after scarcely two hours of ferocious combat, in which the patriots suffered the loss of two of its best generals: Cedeño and Plaza, killed in action, Bolívar won a great victory. Of the 6500 men of the enemy forces only about 2000 were able to escape to Puerto Cabello, together with La Torre and his second in command, General Morales. Also two battalions, totaling about 1000 men under the command of Lieutenant Colonel Tello, who prior to the battle had been sent to San Felipe, upon hearing of the defeat at Carabobo, took refuge at Puerto Cabello. The remaining 3500 represented casualties in dead, wounded and captured. The patriots reported in the official communique only about 200 dead, but undoubtedly their losses were greater. The patriots' army occupied Valencia the same night, and on June 28, 1821 Bolívar made his triumphal entry into Caracas.

Before their defeat at Carabobo this Spanish army, now reduced to about 3000 men who had taken refuge at Puerto Cabello, had been considered the strongest in Spanish America. Through its privileged central position it constituted a menace to all of the other colonies, and its destruction was felt immediately in the entire Spanish American continent. On September 15, 1821 all of the Central American Countries declared their independence, and a week later the independence of Mexico was consummated. Of course, a contributing factor was also the political chaos in Spain.

In Colombia, Cartagena was conquered on October 10th and Cumaná on the 16th, while on the 28th of November Panama proclaimed its independence and its incorporation into Colombia.

To appraise properly the gigantic task of the Liberator and his feverish activity while preparing for Carabobo, the author, who many years ago crossed Colombia on horseback from the Pacific to the Atlantic, visiting the Bolívar battlefields, has made a rough estimate of the distances the Liberator covered in the period of the twenty-two and a half months elapsed between Boyacá and Carabobo. During this period Bolívar, on horseback, crossed and crisscrossed the Andes several times between Bogotá, in the heart of Colombia, and the plains of Venezuela and Angostura. These peregrinations of the Liberator, sometimes accompanied by only a few officers, but more often while mobilizing large contingents of troops, are approximately equivalent, in the distance covered in those twenty-two and a half months, to that between New York City on the North and Buenos Aires, Argentina. This was accomplished by Bolívar through impassable mule trails and, while on the rivers of the interior, by using the extremely primitive means of fluvial transportation prevailing there a century and a half ago.

The First Constitutional Congress was inaugurated at the City of Cúcuta on May 6, 1821, attended by representatives of the nineteen liberated provinces. On June 6th the union of Venezuela and Colombia was ratified under a Central System of Government, at which time Bolívar was elected President and General Santander was elected Vice President.

In recognition of the battle of Carabobo, the Congress decreed the highest honors to the victors, and ordered the portrait of Bolívar placed in their main assembly room with the inscription:

SIMÓN BOLÍVAR
LIBERATOR OF COLOMBIA

General Páez was made General in Chief of the Army, as recommended by the Liberator in recognition of his great bravery at Carabobo, mainly responsible for the victory; and for the troops it was decreed that they wear on the left arm a gold escutcheon surmounted by a laurel wreath, bearing the inscription:

Liberation of Venezuela

CONQUEROR AT CARABOBO—YEAR XI.

The Carabobo victory crowned eleven years of the struggle for independence, starting in Caracas on April 19, 1810.

Two glorious words are engraved in gold in the two countries:

In Colombia: BOYACÁ

In Venezuela: CARABOBO

CHAPTER VIII

Liberation of Ecuador

THE Liberator remained in Caracas scarcely one month, during which time he displayed unusual activity in the reorganization of the government, and while working on this task he ordered all of the properties of the patriots that had been confiscated by the Spaniards restored to the legitimate owners. It was then, upon learning that Don Francisco Iturbe (the Spaniard who had saved his life in 1812—see end of Chapter II) was living penniless in exile because his properties had been automatically confiscated by the Republic when he emigrated to Curacao, that Bolívar addressed a communication to the Congress on August 2, 1821 in which he said in part:

> "If the properties of Don Francisco Iturbe must be confiscated, I offer mine instead, as he offered his life for mine; and if the Sovereign Congress wishes to grant me this favor, my own properties are the ones benefited by it; I am the winner."

The Congress, gratified with this manifestation of respect to the people's representatives, and at the same time admiring Bolívar's behavior, ordered the restitution of Iturbe's properties.

Before leaving Caracas on August 2, 1821 Bolívar issued a proclamation in which he partly said:

> "Caraqueños:—The General Congress with its wisdom has given you laws for your happiness. The liberating army with

its military virtues has returned you to the fatherland. You are now free.

"The union of Venezuela, Cundinamarca and Quito has added new strength to your political life and cemented forever your stability.

"Caraqueños:—Pay the homage of your admiration to the heroes who have created Colombia."

While at Maracaibo, on his way to Bogotá, Bolívar received the news of his unanimous reelection as President of Colombia by the Cúcuta Congress. He immediately proceeded to that city, arriving on September 22, 1821. On October 3rd, upon taking the oath of office of President, in addressing the Congress the Liberator said in part:

"I am the son of war. The man whom the battles have elevated to the executive power of the government. Fortune has favored me in this rank, and victory has confirmed it. But these are not the titles consecrated by justice, happiness and by the National consent. . . . A man like me is a dangerous citizen in a popular government; he is an immediate threat to the national sovereignty. I want to be a citizen to secure my own freedom and the freedom of all. I prefer the title of citizen to that of Liberator, because the latter comes from war, and the former comes from the law. Change, I beg you, all my titles for that of good citizen!"

Bolívar at this time notified the Congress, as he had done before in Angostura, renouncing all of his salaries in favor of the Treasury. In the resolution of the Congress, abiding by his wishes, there is the following paragraph:—

"But he can never refuse the national gratitude which is his best patrimony."

Bolívar arrived in Bogotá three weeks later. While he was there two events favorable to the patriots occurred. The island of Margarita, in eastern Venezuela, had been fully reoccupied on October 16, 1821 by General Bermúdez, and Panamá had declared its independence on November 28, 1821.

Since Caracas, the Liberator had been preparing a campaign to liberate the southern area of Colombia, for which purpose he began mobilizing some troops from Valencia and Maracaibo to be joined with others from Cúcuta and Bogotá. On December 13th having completed his military preparations, the Liberator left Bogotá on his way to Popayán via Cali. While at this latter city he issued a proclamation, on January 17, 1822, to the inhabitants of the Cauca Valley, where both Cali and Popayán are situated in the southern part of Colombia which read in part:

"Colombians of the South:—The liberating army comes to bring you peace and freedom.

"Caucanos:—The day of your reward has arrived. The heroism of your sacrifices insures forever your happiness; it will be the heritage of your children, the benefit of your glory.

"Pastusos:—(Inhabitants of the Province of Pasto, south of Popayán). You have cost tears and shackles to the south; but Colombia forgets its sufferings and consoles itself by bringing back to her bosom her unfortunate children. For Colombia all are innocent; none is guilty. Do not be afraid; the arms of Colombia are for your protection; they are not for your punishment.

"Quiteños:—The Colombian troops are marching toward the ancient Temple of the Sun. Place in them your confidence. Pretty soon you will see its flags unfurled by the Angel of Victory."

Liberation of Ecuador

It was at Popayán, where Bolívar arrived eight weeks after leaving Bogotá that he offered the predominant Spanish colony of the region the protection of the Republic, saying on February 18, 1822 in part:

"Spaniards! If you behave as good citizens you will be treated with unlimited generosity; but if you persist in your stubborn hostility, beware of the rigor of the war laws!"

Bolívar's original plan was to transport his troop contingents by sea from the Pacific port of Buenaventura to Guayaquil in order to liberate Quito, thus avoiding the difficult land transportation through the southern Andes of Colombia, where the City of Pasto is situated, which was a region of arch-royalist fanatics, enemies of the Republic. In short, his plan was to by-pass Pasto until his main objective of conquering Quito, in Ecuador, had been attained. However, disturbing news which he received compelled him to modify these plans. Apparently two powerful Spanish men-of-war were reported navigating in the vicinity of the Colombian coast. As Bolívar had no armed ships available to protect his troop convoys, he had no alternative but to march his troops to Quito, through the valley of the Patía River and the Andean region of Pasto.

The difficulties encountered by the Liberator in this herculean feat were incredible. The district of the river valley of Patía, located scarcely one degree North of the Equator, possessed one of the most deadly climates of the tropics. The area was plagued with malaria, dysentery, diarrhea, hookworm, smallpox and other tropical diseases, besides the scourge of swarms of locusts. The inhabitants of this inhospitable region were mostly descendents of negro slaves and, banded together in criminal gangs organized as guerrillas under the royalist banners, committed all kinds of depredations. It was unsafe to travel through that region at any season of the year. Beyond Patía, the Juanambú River region had to be crossed—a torrential stream in a deep chasm of the Andes, which for the few scattered Spanish garrisons defending the district provided an almost impregnable natural barrier for the movement of troops. On the other side of the Juanambú River there was a strip of woods, very abrupt and almost impassable, extending between that river and another torrential mountain stream, the Guáitara. In this region of overpowering mountain gorges, always covered by dense fog, a few soldiers from the Spanish troops garrisoned at Pasto could stop an entire army.

Between the Juanambú and the Guáitara Rivers stood the City of Pasto, at an elevation of 8,600 feet, on the slopes of the Galera Volcano, a mighty giant of the Andes, with its peak crowned by perpetual snows. The natives of Pasto, perhaps as a result of their isolation from the rest of the country, were extremely hostile to the Colombian cause. In all of the Americas they were the most fanatic, energetic, brave and loyal subjects of the King. The Pasto population were ready at all times to sacrifice their personal possessions and their lives in defense of their King and their religion.

Some fifty miles southwest of Pasto the battle of Bombobná took place on April 7, 1822. It had taken Bolívar's army nearly two months to cross the territory between Popayán and Pasto, a distance which in a straight line, as the crow flies, might scarcely represent one hundred miles. However, crossing over the abrupt Andes, interspersed with deep ravines and torrential mountain streams, along the precarious mule trails which Bolívar's troops had to follow, the distance was three times as great. When the troops left Popayán they totaled some 2850 men. Only 1800 survived to arrive at Bombobná. One thousand men had been lost in the devastating march, through disease and desertions. Furthermore, the army was continuously harassed by guerrillas whom the Spaniards had placed in strategic points along the route. Bombloná, the name of a small farm, is located at the bottom of a gully. Bolívar's army had at its right the torrential Guáitara. This river, through which a wide and swift current flowed over perpendicularly cut rocks, could not be crossed except through two bridges, which were strongly fortified by the enemy. To the left the patriots had the forbidding Galera Volcano, about 16,000 feet high, and directly facing them stood the Cariaco hill, a slope of Galera, on the top of which was intrenched the Spanish army 2200 strong, under the command of Colonel Basilio García, a veteran of Morillo's army. In order to reach the hill the patriots had first to cross over a small bridge on the Cariaco stream, which was crisscrossed by enemy fire from the infantry as well as by two cannons placed there. This bridge and the Cariaco hill led directly to Pasto.

The battle which lasted six hours, was won by Bolívar but only after suffering 450 casualties in dead and wounded, including, among the former, General Torres.* Spanish Colonel García escaped to Pasto with an escort of only sixty soldiers, under cover of the darkness of the night. The remainder of his defeated troops took shelter through the surrounding territory and could not be pursued by the patriots after darkness due to the abruptness of the terrain. The Spaniards' losses were only about 250 in dead, wounded and prisoners.

Bolívar has been greatly criticized by several historians, including that great biographer of the Liberator, Dr. Vicente Lecuna, who wrote that "Bombloná was a lamentable mistake

---

* General Pedro Leon Torres, born in the Province of Caracas in 1790; died August 22, 1822 at Yaquanquer from his wounds at Bombloná. Upon receiving news of the death of Torres, Bolívar is reported to have said: "With his death we have lost a comrade deserving our love; the army a soldier of great merit; and the Republic one of its men of hope for the day of peace." At Bombloná, Torres was 32 years old.

—to have engaged the enemy with inferior forces and through a frontal attack."

I respect Dr. Lecuna's opinions and consider him my best teacher and mentor on Bolívar. Together we visited, on the occasion of the Ayacucho Centennial, the battlefields of both Junin and Ayacucho. However, Dr. Lecuna, personally, was never at Bomboná, a site to which I made a pilgrimage while visiting nearby Berruecos, where General Sucre was assassinated. In my opinion Bolívar's army was trapped at Bomboná. Any other General, lacking his genius and impetuosity of character, would have tried to withdraw rather than to engage from an inferior position the formidable intrenched enemy. This withdrawal, however, would have meant total annihilation at the hands of the Spaniards. There was no alternative for Bolívar except to attack. And this he did. Although in his frontal attack, which Dr. Lecuna criticizes, his losses were enormous, he succeeded in defeating the enemy. General Manuel Antonio López (at the time a Lieutenant) who participated in the battle, narrates in his memoirs that in order to reach the strong battlements of the enemy at the top of the Cariaco hill, the Bolívar soldiers had to anchor themselves on the steep embankment by sticking their bayonets into the ground.

While the defeated enemy troops began taking refuge at Pasto, Bolívar, having lost one fourth of his army, retraced his steps and led his troops to Mercaderes, about 75 miles from Pasto. Here he belatedly received, on May 26, 1822, the reinforcements he had repeatedly urgently requested from Bogotá. With these, his army was again increased to 2000 men.

Let us momentarily leave the Liberator at Mercaderes and briefly explain the important events that meanwhile had transpired in Guayaquil and Quito, the territory now comprising the Republic of Ecuador, the ultimate goal of Bolívar and his troops.

A year and a half before, on October 9, 1820, the citizens of Guayaquil had deposed the Spanish authorities and proclaimed their independence. Informed of this, Bolívar, then at Bogotá, had sent to Guayaquil one of his aides-de-camp, General Mires to greet and congratulate the new Government. And on January 21, 1821, the Liberator had sent General Sucre with troops to Guayaquil to open a campaign against the royalist divisions. At the time Sucre received these orders he had been acting as Chief of Operations in southern Colombia.

On April 4, 1821 Sucre set sail for Guayaquil from the Pacific Colombian Port of Buenaventura with 400 troops, arriving at his destination one month later. On May 7th, Sucre presented himself before the Council governing the city and after seven weeks, having succeeded in organizing there an army corps, he left Guayaquil on June 29, 1821, on his way to conquer Quito.

After a victory at Yaguachi and a disastrous defeat at Guachi, Sucre was soon back at Guayaquil to reorganize his defeated troops. Mobilizing again his contingents toward Quito he received, while at Ona, on February 16, 1822, strong reinforcements which he had previously requested from the Peruvian Government. With these, together with some additional troops sent from Guayaquil, Sucre had under his command about 2200 infantry and 400 cavalry, or a total of about 2600 men. On his way to Quito, Sucre took the Cities of Riobamba and Ambato, arriving at La Tacunga on May 2, 1822, where Colombian Colonel Córdova joined him with 200 troops from Bogotá.

On May 24th 1822 on the slopes of the mighty Pichincha Volcano, (crowned by four snowcapped peaks, about 16,000 feet high), and facing the Valley of Quito, Sucre's army defeated the enemy under Colonel Nicolás López, 2500 strong and the next day occupied the City of Quito. Here, its Governor, Spanish General Aymerich, surrendered the remnants of his troops to Sucre after capitulation. As a result of the glorious victory 1300 soldiers plus 160 officers were taken prisoners. Fourteen pieces of artillery, 1700 rifles, plus all of the Spanish army impedimenta were captured by the patriots. On the battle field (*about 9500* feet high) 400 Spaniards and 200 patriots died; the casualties of Sucre's army were 140 wounded. The magnificent victory of Pichincha not only assured the independence of Ecuador but of Colombia as well. Sucre was then twentynine years old. Five days after the battle, the Municipality of Quito spontaneously proclaimed in public session the incorporation with Colombia of the former Kingdom of Quito.

We had left the Liberator with a force of 2000 men at Mercaderes, seventyfive miles from the City of Pasto, on May 26th, two days after Sucre had defeated the Spaniards at Pichincha. Greatly strengthened with the reinforcements he had received, Bolívar proposed capitulation to the Spanish Commander, which the latter received at Pasto, at the same time as the news of the defeat of the royalists at Pichincha. A Spanish military Junta quickly accepted the proposed terms of surrender, although this was contrary to the wishes of the inhabitants of the city, whose desire was to continue fighting the patriots.

Upon being informed of the acceptance of his terms, the Liberator, who had already received the glad tidings about Pichincha, hastened his departure, in advance of that of his troops and, surrounded by only a few officers and soldiers, entered Pasto on the afternoon of June 6th. On June 8, 1822, while at Pasto,* he issued a proclamation in which he said in part:

"Colombians:—Your beautiful fatherland is now free. The victories of Bomboná and Pichincha have completed the task of your heroism. From the shores of the Orinoco to the Andes of Peru, the liberating army, marching in triumph, has covered with its protecting arms all of the Colombian territory. Only one stronghold resists but we will conquer it.

"Colombians of the south:—The blood of your brothers has redeemed you of the horrors of war.

". . . Colombians:—I want you to partake of the oceans of joy that fill my heart and to place in yours the liberating army that has given you glory, peace and freedom."

From Pasto, Bolívar crossed the Ecuadorian border and on June 12th at the City of Ibarra, he was welcomed by Colonel José María Córdova, one of the heroes of Pichincha, who had been sent by Sucre with a battalion of troops to Pasto.

On June 15, 1822 the Liberator made his triumphal entry into the City of Quito, among the tumultuous enthusiasm and general joy of its 40,000 inhabitants, who had decorated their windows and balconies with garlands of flowers.

* Pasto was to continue to be a source of concern for the Liberator. Scarcely four months later, an insurrection of the Pastusos against the Republic flared up, which General Sucre, sent there with some troops by Bolívar, was only able to subdue by Christmas 1822. Six months later a second revolt erupted, with the Pastusos invading the neighboring Ecuadorean City of Ibarra. Bolívar had to quell this in person and to prevent further trouble he imposed severe measures against the stubborn population of Pasto. He not only ordered the forced conscription of all available men into the battalions then being sent to Peru but also the exile of their families to Guayaquil.

After Pichincha, Sucre was promoted by Bolívar to Major General and was appointed Governor of the Southern Department, which comprised the territory of the present Republic of Ecuador.

As our story will soon take us to the neighboring country of Perú, we have to digress a little and go back to the year 1821, when on July 28 the victorious Argentine and Chilean armies under General José de San Martín invaded Perú and declared its independence. San Martín assumed then the title of "Protector of Peru." One of San Martín's preoccupations at the time was to bring as part of the Peruvian territory the northern province of Guayaquil, Ecuador, which, although politically was administered by the Spanish Presidency of Quito, militarily had been under the jurisdiction of the former Spanish Viceroyalty of Perú.

A few months before the invasion of Perú by the San Martín armies, the citizens of Guayaquil had declared their independence from Spain and when San Martín arrived in Lima he lost no time in sending to Guayaquil three Commissioners to negotiate the incorporation of that Province to Perú. These ambitious plans, however, clashed with those of Bolívar who, since the Congress at Angostura, was determined to bring into Colombia the Provinces of Quito and Guayaquil. In furtherance of his plans, Bolívar, after a stay in Quito of scarcely two weeks, left for Guayaquil, arriving on July 11, 1822. The Government of the Province, influenced by the intrigues of the San Martín Commissioners, was inclined toward union with Perú. However, the great statesmanship and popularity of the Liberator, plus his victories of Bomboná and Pichincha, swayed overnight the public sentiment in favor of annexation to Colombia.

Alarmed with these developments, San Martín decided to leave for Guayaquil on July 14, 1822, appointing as head of the Peruvian Government during his absence the Marquis de Torre Tagle, with the title of Supreme Delegate. San Martín arrived at Guayaquil on the 26th of July, at which time he and Bolívar held a long conference. This was resumed on the following day and lasted for several hours. On the evening of the 27th San Martín embarked on his way back to Peru, and two months later, on September 20, 1822, he resigned his position as head of the Peruvian Government and sailed for Chile, into exile, never to return to the two countries he had helped to liberate.

There were no witnesses to the two interviews between San Martín and Bolívar. However, from documents published later it is inferred that the two liberators exchanged views over the future of Guayaquil and that the genius and intellectual superiority of Bolívar prevailed. Four days after the departure of San Martín from Guayaquil, the Electoral Assembly of the Province unanimously declared all of its territory to be part of Colombia.

When San Martín resigned his command in Peru and went into exile he left in the country over 11,000 troops of Argentine, Chilean and Peruvian contingents, under the command of Argentine Generals Alvarado and Arenales. This force was superior in numbers and equipment to that of the Spaniards. San Martín was confident that with this superiority over the enemy his subordinates would have no difficulty in completing his task of liberating the country.

However, contrary to the expectations of the "Protector of Perú," several military disasters were suffered by the united army at the hands of the Spaniards. With San Martín gone, the Peruvian Government turned to Bolívar, asking for the help of Colombia in men and equipment. This was immediately given and the Liberator lost no time in sending to Perú, between the middle of March 1823 and that of May, several contingents of Colombian troops properly trained and equipped, totaling in all about 6000 men, but due mostly to sickness only 5500 arrived at their destination. On April 14, 1823 Bolívar sent General Sucre to Lima as his special representative before the Peruvian Government.

But the Peruvian authorities in addition to asking for troops also wanted Bolívar to come to Lima, believing him to be the only man who could save their country. For this purpose two Peruvian envoys arrived in Guayaquil on April 26, 1823. The Liberator, however, as President of Colombia, could not leave the country without special authorization of the Colombian Congress, which Bolívar immediately requested. Meanwhile, since the political and military situation in Peru had become exceedingly critical, the Peruvian Congress on May 14th approved a resolution of thanks to the Liberator for his military help and urged him to come personally to their assistance. This was followed on June 19th 1823 by the sending to Guayaquil of two special envoys from the Congress, which was then assembled at Callao, as Lima, the Capital, had been occupied by the enemy. These envoys were José Joaquin Olmedo and José Sánchez Carrión.

The envoys met the Liberator at Quito, where he had just returned from Pasto. Olmedo, in presenting their credentials and addressing the Liberator, urging him to come to Perú, said when describing the vast resources and wealth of that country:

"We have everything but need a voice to unite us; a hand to guide us, and a genius to take us to victory."

On August 2, 1823 Bolívar received Congressional authorization to go to Perú, which had been granted at Bogotá on June 4th. It had taken two months, via Buenaventura, to reach him at Guayaquil. On August 7, 1823, on the glorious anniversary of the battle of Boyacá, the Liberator embarked at Guayaquil for Peru on an adventure which was going to try his tenacity and creative genius to the utmost; that was to deplete his vitality and undermine his health to such an extent that after this trying period he never fully regained his strength. This venture was in a way responsible for his premature death, seven years later. However, he was able to attain in Perú the goal he had set for himself earlier in life— the liberation of a Continent, crowned by some of the most glorious victories mankind has ever known.

CHAPTER IX

Liberation of Perú

WHILE these events were taking place in Ecuador and Perú, Spanish General Francisco Morales, surrendered the remnants of his troops at Maracaibo on August 3, 1823, thus ending forever Spanish domination in Venezuela.

The situation which the Liberator found upon his arrival in Lima on September 1, 1823, could not have been more calamitous. In the short period of one year, since San Martín had left the country, the excellent military organization left by the Protector had almost vanished. The country was bankrupt and the political situation in a pitiful state of chaos. President Riva Agüero, who had been deposed by the Congress, insisted on governing by decree from the northern City of Trujillo, while the Peruvian legislative body, assembled in Lima, had appointed a new President, the Marquis de Torre Tagle. Riva Agüero was supported in the north by a few Peruvian battalions, while the Congress at Lima had none, and their only hope was the Colombian troops sent by the Liberator.

These internal dissensions, verging on civil war, were taking place in the face of the Spanish enemy, with an army of over 20,000 men intrenched from Jauja (Peruvian Andes) to Potosí (Bolivia), occupying most of the Peruvian territory, except for a small coastal strip between Callao and the North, plus the Andean valleys of Huánuco.

The day after Bolívar arrived in Lima, greeted by the delirious enthusiasm of the population, who received him as a saviour, one of the first acts of the Congress was to invest him with the necessary authority to end the division of the Government with Riva Agüero. This mission Bolívar accepted reluctantly. However, when subsequently informed that the Congress wanted to appoint him Supreme Dictator, the Liberator sent that body a communication in which he expressed his aversion to meddling in the civilian affairs of the country, limiting his services to the military. He said in part:

"I, Your Excellency, left Bogotá to seek the enemies of America, wherever they may be, and these are yet to be found in the territory of Perú. I abandoned the Capital of Colombia to avoid, so to speak, civilian authority. My aversion to engaging in the Administration of the Government defies exaggeration, and thus I have renounced forever any civil power that may have no direct connection with military operations. I will better explain it—I have retained that part of the Government that contributes, like gunpowder, to the destruction of our enemies. With this thought, I again offer the Peruvian Congress my active coöperation for the salvation of their fatherland; but this offer is limited only to the use of my sword."

In spite of this, the Congress invested the Liberator, on September 10, 1823, with Supreme Military Authority, together with the ordinary and extraordinary powers that the critical situation of the country demanded. In reality, this was a true dictatorship because although Torre Tagle remained as nominal President of the Republic, his powers were a shadow of those conferred upon Bolívar.

On September 13th the Liberator, appearing before Congress, said in part:

"The liberating soldiers that have come from the River Plate, the Maule River (in Chile), the Magdalena (in

97

Colombia) and the Orinoco (in Venezuela), will return to their countries covered with laurels, under triumphal arches and carrying as trophies the flags of Castille. They will conquer and will leave a free Perú, or all will die. I promise you!"

Then the Liberator said to the President of the Congress:

"Sir, I offer you victory, trusting in the courage of the United Army, and in the good faith of the Congress, the Executive Power, and the Peruvian people. Thus Perú will be free and remain sovereign and independent for all of the centuries that Divine Providence may decree."

One month later the Congress, on information that Ex-President Riva Agüero, from Trujillo, was negotiating with the enemy, declared him a traitor and ordered him apprehended. It was at this time that a great military disaster occurred in southern Perú. A Peruvian army, 5000 strong, under the command of General Santa Cruz, who had left Callao four months before to fight the Spaniards in the south, was practically annihilated by the enemy.

As the few Peruvian battalions, yet faithful to Riva Agüero, were stationed in the northern Provinces of Huaraz and Trujillo, the Liberator decided to place his Colombian troops between the Peruvian contingents and the Spaniards, thus cutting off their communications and then attack the Peruvian insurgents. On November 11th, Bolívar left Lima for Supe, a port about 180 miles to the north. On the 16th, upon mobilizing his troops, he issued a proclamation to them in which he said:

". . . Colombian Soldiers:—A Congress of the Representatives of the people, supported only by the national determination, but without troops or military power, fights an unequal contest against a rebel army. No! Colombians! From the end of the world you would come to save the law, the liberty of Perú. March immediately to punish any and all that may try in future to imitate the monster Riva Agüero." ". . . Soldiers:—Always defend with your rifles and bayonets the laws of liberty and you will be unconquerable!"

At Huaraz the Colombian troops were divided in two. Some were under the command of General Sucre and went to the south to face the Spaniards up to the Andean knot of Pasco, 14,350 feet high; the others, under Bolívar's command went to the north to Cajamarca to pursue the Riva Agüero battalions.

The plan of the Liberator was to station the Colombian contingents under Sucre's command in the Provinces of Huánuco and Huamachuco in the valleys to the east of the White Cordillera. Others, in the Callejón de Huaylas, between the Black and White Cordilleras; while the cavalry was garrisoned toward the coast. It was Bolívar's foresight to acclimate the troops to the rarefied air of the mountains in the country where they were to fight the enemy. It was the beginning of a task of preparation carried out with insurmountable patience, brilliance and energy, which was later to be crowned with the most splendid victories of American Independence.

On November 25th, Riva Agüero and his Minister of War, Herrera, were captured and sent into exile, while the Liberator, traveling from Pasco to Cajamarca, through Huaraz to Huamachuco, succeeded without firing a single shot in obtaining the surrender of the remnants of the Riva Agüero troops, who again yielded to the Lima Government. Thus

ended the abortive attempt at civil war. Also, two followers
of Riva Agüero, General Santa Cruz and Vice Admiral Guise,
upon hearing the news of the exile of their former chief, placed
themselves again under Bolívar's command.

After the surrender of the Peruvian troops, Bolívar, while
on his way back to Lima from Trujillo, fell seriously ill at
Pativilca. He had to remain there for one month, during
which time he was unable even to mount a horse. It was
while at Pativilca that the Liberator received news of another
great disaster, which placed in jeopardy his carefully laid
plans, testing to the utmost his iron will and sterling determination to save the country. On February 5, 1824, the Argentine troops garrisoned at Callao, due to lack of pay and
deficient food, revolted under a mulatto (Sergeant Moyano)
and after imprisoning their officers, delivered the forts to the
enemy.

Five days after this treachery the Peruvian Congress invested Bolívar with unlimited powers and asked him to save
the Republic. But Congress had placed on Bolívar's shoulders
a veritable corpse. The Treasury was empty. Public opinion
was disgusted with the cause of independence, and most of
the Peruvian army was totally demoralized and bankrupt. The
ships of the small Peruvian navy were in great need of repair
and its crews had been unpaid for a year. Meanwhile the
enemy's armies, with bounteous resources were occupying excellent positions.

Bolívar, in view of the circumstances, reluctantly accepted
these new overwhelming responsibilities, and on February 13,
1824 he issued the following proclamation to the Peruvians:

". . . Peruvians: The circumstances are frightful for
your fatherland; you know it, but do not lose faith in the
Republic. It is dying, but it is still alive. The Colombian

Army is still intact and invincible. We are besides waiting for 10,000 additional braves of the heroes of Colombia who are coming from the fatherland.

". . . Peruvians: In five months we have experienced five treasons and defections; but you still have against one million and a half enemies, fourteen million Americans who will protect you with the shield of their arms. Justice also favors you, and you are fighting in its name. Heaven awards victory to the just!"

And with his feverish activity and superb mastery for even the most minute details, the Liberator wrote General Sucre, in command of the Colombian troops in the north, advising him of the route his divisions should follow, the conditions and requirements necessary for the garrisoning of the troops, the way to deploy the men; how to prepare the shelters in the mountains that were to replace the tents; the way to obtain cattle and food; how the hospitals should be located as well as the ambulances and other war material and impedimenta. He also placed special emphasis on the training of the soldiers and their positions; and, as if it were a chess game, the places that Sucre should occupy with his army, anticipating the movements of their adversaries, and advising him how to act to defeat the enemy.

Subsequently on February 28, 1824 when the enemy reoccupied Lima, another treacherous occurrence took place. President Torre Tagle, his Vice President, his Minister of War and the principal functionaries of the Government, plus 337 officers, including Generals and Colonels, deserted the flags of the fatherland and humiliated themselves before the oppressors.

To fill his cup of bitterness, the loss of Callao and Lima, and the defection to the enemy of the principal government officials and Peruvian Army officers was followed on March 17, 1824 by the desertion at Supe of two Peruvian cavalry commanders with their forces, who went to join the Spaniards. It was in situations like this that he showed himself superior to any adversity. Relying on the vast resources of his genius, which appeared to grow with the obstacles, he knew himself capable of overcoming them.

After this heartrending treason, which perhaps marked the lowest ebb of the Liberator's misfortunes in Perú, he issued the following proclamation to the Peruvians:

"Peruvians:—The disasters of the Army and the conflict of the political parties have reduced Perú to the unfortunate situation of having to resort to the tyrannic powers of a dictator to save itself. Your Congress has conferred upon me this odious authority. . . . I would have preferred never to have come to Perú and would even have chosen your own loss to the frightful title of Dictator. However, as Colombia was bound to your own fate, I have not hesitated."

"Peruvians! Your own officials, your internal enemies have slandered Colombia, its brave army, and even myself. It has been said that we pretend to usurp your rights, your territory, and your independence. I declare to you, in the name of Colombia and in that of the sacred liberating army that my authority will not go beyond the time necessary to prepare ourselves for victory; that the moment the army evacuates the provinces they now occupy, you will be constitutionally governed by your own laws and magistrates."

"Peruvians! The field of battle that will witness the valor of our soldiers, the triumph of our liberty, that fortunate battlefield will see me throw away the cloak of dictatorship, and from there I will return to Colombia with my brothers in arms, without taking with me even a grain of sand from Perú, and leaving with you: Liberty!"

After the loss of Lima, Bolívar established his general headquarters at the northern city of Trujillo, which he declared the provisional capital of Perú. He began by introducing economies in all of the branches of the administration. He eliminated superfluous government positions, reduced the salaries of the remaining employees as well as the soldiers' pay, which up to then had been entirely nominal and which he cut down to one fourth of that prescribed by law. He concentrated in one single Secretary General the handling of all civil and political affairs: José Sánchez Carrión, a Peruvian of great capacity, who thoroughly enjoyed through his exceptional talents and application the confidence of the Liberator.

To acquire funds he persuaded the ecclesiastical authorities to donate to the government the silver and gold vessels of the churches, and confiscated the properties of all those who had deserted to serve the enemy. He created taxes and enforced their collection. Through his enterprising genius, he obtained revenues where none had previously existed. One of his favorite endeavors was public instruction. He established a University at Trujillo and schools in all the areas that he visited.

While he was at Trujillo Bolívar received on March 27, 1824 the news of President Monroe's famous declaration before the North American Congress at Washington, (Monroe's seventh message to the congress on December 12th 1823.) branding any European intervention in the Americas as dangerous and hostile to the U.S.A. This was opportune because France once again, this time allied with Spain, had designs on the Spanish Colonies. Thus the Monroe Doctrine was born.

Bolívar remained at Trujillo scarcely five weeks, during which time the City became transformed into a vast military arsenal where no one was idle. Even the women of Trujillo, including those of high social rank, were busy sewing clothing for the troops. In one month there was obtained a great quantity of clothing and shoes, as well as leather straps and saddles, arms and ammunition, and even horseshoes. For the soldiers' canteen he collected all of the tin plate and wire available for fifty miles around; and being in need of lead for solder, he collected all the nails made of that metal that were being used to bind leather seats to chairs. After this there was not one usable chair left, even in the churches.

The Liberator even took the time to issue minute instructions as to how to manufacture the nails for horseshoes and how to alloy the various metals. However, his greatest attention was concentrated on increasing the discipline of the soldiers. In order to acclimate them to the rarefied air of the high mountains he had the soldiers exercise a march of thirty miles a week over precipitous ground. He instructed his staff in ways to collect cattle and food supplies to be stored at various points of the Andes which were to be crossed by the troops. In this task General Sucre crossed over the high mountain passes three times, in the most inclement weather, exploring the most remote corners of the Cordilleras to select in advance the places that were to provide appropriate shelter for the troops.

On April 22, 1824 Bolívar left Trujillo and during the months of May and June he established his headquarters at Huaraz and Caraz, from which latter point he visited all of the various contingents of his army. It was while at Huaraz, around the middle of the month of July, that he received the visit of U. S. A. Naval Captain Hiram Paulding (afterward Admiral Paulding) who had been sent by Commodore Hull, head of the North American Squadrons of the Pacific. Paulding, writing afterward in his Memoirs about the visit, mentions that when he asked the Liberator about his decision for the cause of independence Bolívar said:

"Since childhood I had that obsession. I was delighted with the history of Greece and Rome. The recent North American Revolution presented a stimulus and an example, and the character of Washington instilled in my heart a desire to emulate him."

Meanwhile internal political dissension among the Spanish generals in Perú, which caused a temporary split of their forces, considerably helped the cause of the patriots. In October of the previous year King Ferdinand of Spain had dissolved Parliament and again had become the Supreme Dictator of the country. This action resulted in a political schism among the Royalists in Perú. Spanish Viceroy of Perú, La Serna, and his two principal Generals, José de Canterac, Chief of the Royalist armies in Perú, and Gerónimo Valdés, his Lieutenant, were in favor of the Spanish Constitution. On the other hand General Pedro Antonio de Olañeta, commanding the Spanish troops in the Provinces of Alto Perú (Bolivia) who was in favor of the absolutism of the King, revolted with his forces against the Viceroy. La Serna from Cuzco, where he had established his temporary headquarters, had sent General Valdés in February 1824, with 5000 troops, to subdue Olañeta. This decision of the Viceroy to split the Spanish forces was to prove fatal to the forthcoming battle of Junín. The Spaniards had at that time in Perú over 20,000 troops, of which 16,000 were engaged in active operations and the remainder in garrisons. General Canterac was quartered with his division of about 7000 men in the valleys around Jauja, located about 100 miles south of Pasco. Some of the other Spanish contingents were with the Viceroy at Cuzco while others were stationed at Lima and Callao, and General Valdés was fighting Olañeta in Upper Perú.

The patriots' contingents had been increased to 8700 troops by the arrival of reinforcements sent by Colombia under General Córdóva and Colonel Miguel Antonio Figueredo. On June 15, 1824 the Liberator ordered the army to cross the Andes through various routes. He, himself, crossed over a pass 16,500 feet high. The entire patriots' army assembled at Cerro de Pasco (14,350 feet above sea level) on August 1st, and on the following day, when reviewing the troops, among which there were men from Caracas, Panamá, Quito, Lima, Chile, Buenos Aires and some British soldiers, the Liberator issued the following proclamation:

"Soldiers:—You are going to complete the greatest task that Heaven has ever entrusted to man: that of delivering a whole world from slavery.

"Soldiers! The enemies whom you are going to destroy boast of fourteen years of victories; thus they will be worthy of crossing their arms with yours, which have excelled in a thousand combats . . .

"Soldiers! Perú and all America expect from you peace, the daughter of victory; and even liberal Europe gazes upon you with delight because the liberty of the New World is the hope of the Universe. Will you betray it? No! No! You are invincible!"

And he reminded the Colombians of various glorious battle names saying:

"Soldiers! The hope of nations depends upon your bravery. On this same month you have triumphed at Cara-

cas and at Boyacá: Add a new day of glory to your fatherland."

Colonel O'Connor, who participated in many of the battles
of the South American Independence, and who was with the
Liberator in Perú and Bolivia, wrote many years later in his
memoirs:

"The tone of his voice was soft and pleasant; harsh in his
moments of anger, and seemed to acquire the roar of
thunder when issuing his proclamations or giving orders on
the battlefield." And he added: "And I still remember his
gaze, full of fire, haughty and penetrating."

Spanish General Canterac had moved his troops to the
north in the area of the high and desolate tableland of Junín,
at an altitude of 14,000 feet. However, leaving the major part
of his army behind, he advanced with his cavalry toward
Pasco to obtain information on Bolivar's movements. Arriving at Pasco on August 5th, and finding that the patriots'
army had vanished, Canterac hastily retraced his steps in an
endeavor to elude Bolívar and seek shelter further south.
However, at four o'clock in the afternoon of August 6th, the
vanguard of Bolívar's army, reaching the crest of the hills overlooking Junín, detected the enemy about three miles away on
the plain, in full retreat toward the south. About five o'clock
the Bolívar riders began to reach the plain, with the sun already low on the horizon.

Canterac, discovering the cavalry squadrons of Bolívar, 900
strong, rushing down the hills through a narrow opening and
in a difficult position, considered the situation propitious and
instructed his own cavalry, 1300 strong, to attack the patriots
before they had time to form into battle on the plain. The

fight lasted less than an hour, or until darkness. It was the most important battle engagement of the wars of independence in Spanish America, fought in hand to hand combat, where not a single shot was fired. The Bolívar llaneros, armed with lances ten to eleven feet long (the Spanish lances measured only six to seven feet) decided the affray in favor of the patriots and soon destroyed the careful formation of the enemy squadrons, cutting them to pieces. Colonel O'Connor, who participated in the battle, wrote:

"The charges of our llaneros made the earth tremble."

The losses to the enemy were 12 officers and 245 soldiers killed, a great number wounded and many desertions. The patriots' loss was 45 dead and 99 wounded. Of the latter, Argentine General Necochea, Commander of the Cavalry Squadrons, received seven wounds. The patriots collected an enormous booty in arms and impedimenta, plus 80 prisoners and 400 saddled horses. At Junín, the enemy's cavalry was reduced to one third, and its infantry suffered a great number of desertions, abandoning their equipment while in flight.

Spanish General García Camba, who fought at Ayacucho under Viceroy La Serna, wrote in his memoirs in 1846 on the battle of Junín:

"The superb Spanish Army that at the beginning of August was full of fire, is in the most dejected condition after Junín."

After his victory at Junín, Bolívar issued the following proclamation:

"Peruvians! . . . The Canterac Army has received at Junín a mortal blow, having lost as a result one third of its forces and all of its moral strength . . .

"Peruvians: . . . Pretty soon we will visit the cradle of the Peruvian Empire and the Temple of the Sun. Cuzco will have on the first day of its liberty more joy and glory than under the golden rule of the Incas."

Three days after Junín, the Liberator, witnessing the precipitous flight of the enemy toward Cuzco, abandoning in their wake the rich Provinces of Tarma, Jauja and Huancayo, ordered Colonel Luís Urdaneta, Commander General of the Coastal territory to organize rapidly a division, with part of the soldiers released from the hospitals, and some guerrillas, and retake Lima and Callao. With 1200 troops Urdaneta occupied Lima and then proceeded to the siege of Callao.

Simultaneously, Canterac, after his defeat at Junín, with his army reduced to less than 5000 abandoned the Provinces of Huamanga, Andahuaylas and Huarmey, and rushed toward Cuzco to join the Viceroy there. On September 14, 1824, he established his headquarters on the other side of the Apurímac River, at Limatambo, about thirty miles from Cuzco. A week later, the patriots' army, after occupying Tarma and Huancayo, entered the City of Huamanga (Ayacucho).

Meanwhile urgent business claimed Bolívar's presence at the Coast. The Colombian Government notified him that they were sending him 3000 troops, of the 12,000 he had requested, which were already on their way to Perú. At the same time he received the disturbing news of the arrival in Peruvian waters of the Spanish Man-of-War "Asia" and the Brigantine "Aquiles," thus endangering the sea communications between Colombia and Perú. He was also informed of the defeat of the

Spanish General Olañeta by the forces of Valdés at La Lava, forty miles from Potosí (Bolívia) which permitted the Valdés forces to rejoin those of Canterac. Thus, after appointing General Sucre on October 6, 1824 Commander in Chief of the army during his absence, Bolívar left for Lima arriving at Andahuaylas on the 10th, and at Huancayo on the 24th. At this latter city he received the disheartening news of the cancellation by the Colombian Congress of his extraordinary powers, and at the same time he was informed of a third insurrection at Pasto. Bolívar entered Lima on November 7, 1824, and with the help of some Colombian troops that had arrived from Panamá, intensified the siege of Callao. From Chancay, a port thirtysix miles north of Lima, he wrote with prophetic vision, on November 10th, to José Manuel Restrepo; at Bogota:—

"In less than a year since I left Lima, I have retaken fifteen Provinces that were in the hands of the dissidents, and liberated more than twenty under the Spanish oppressors. I have achieved this without firing a single shot. From Tumbes (on the Peruvian border with Ecuador) to the Apurímac River (in the Cuzco Valley) Perú has been liberated from anarchy and tyranny; we have buried the civil war. The New Year will witness peace born from the last cannon shot, and there will no longer be any Spaniards in America."

Scarcely a month later this prophecy was to be fulfilled with the triumph at Ayacucho, which liberated Perú and ended forever Spanish domination in South America.

On his long trek of about 800 miles, between Potosí and Cuzco Spanish General Gerónimo Valdés lost two fifths of his division and thus joined the forces of Canterac with only 3000 men. Viceroy La Serna, upon receiving these additional troops, immediately mobilized them to avenge Junín. His forces then totaled about 11,200 men. After a series of marches and counter marches for a distance of about 250 miles between the Apurimac affluents and Huamanga (Ayacucho) during which the patriots' and the Spanish armies were practically facing each other, they reached the Ayacucho battlefield on December 8, 1824.

The Spaniards, 9310 strong, were encamped on the slopes of Mount Condorcunca, facing the Ayacucho tableland, while General Sucre's troops, 5780 strong, were located on the plateau. On the next day, December 9th, the battle was fought. Outnumbered by the enemy, nearly two to one, Sucre's superb strategy gave him the victory. By preventing the Spaniards from entering the plain with all of their forces, he proceeded to cut them piecemeal, destroying first their center and left flank and then, at the crucial moment when 3000 Spaniards of their right flank, under the command of General Valdés, were sweeping away the Peruvian Division opposing them, Sucre threw against this sudden onslaught all of his reserve battalions, routing the enemy in confusion. Victory was achieved in scarcely over two hours. At Ayacucho, Sucre was thirtyone years old. (For a superb description of the battle, we recommend a book by Dr. Vicente Lecuna, published at Caracas in 1941, entitled "Campañas de Junín y Ayacucho.")

Ayacucho was the final battle of the wars of independence on the American Continent. The booty was immense: all of the arms, ammunition and baggage of the Spanish army. In addition, the patriots captured two Lieutenant Generals, including the Viceroy; four Field Marshals; ten Brigadier Generals; sixteen Colonels; 68 Lieutenant Colonels; 484 Majors and Commissioned Officers, plus over 2000 soldiers. The Spaniard's casualties were 1800 dead and 700 wounded, while the patriots' losses were only 310 dead and 609 wounded. Sucre, on that same day, while still on the battlefield arranged a capitulation, under most generous terms, which surrendered the entire territory of Perú.

On receiving in Lima the news of the battle of Ayacucho, the Liberator issued the following proclamation on December 25, 1824:

"Soldiers: . . . You have liberated South America and one fourth of the world is the monument to your glory. Where have you not conquered? . . .

"Soldiers: Colombia owes to you the glory that you have again given her; Perú its life, its liberty and its peace. . . .

"Soldiers: Receive the unbounded gratitude that I offer you in the name of Perú. I equally offer you that you will be rewarded as you deserve before you return to your beautiful fatherland. But No! You will never be worthily rewarded! Your services are priceless!

"Peruvian Soldiers: . . . Your fatherland will always cherish you among the first Liberators of Perú.

"Colombian Soldiers: Hundreds of victories proclaim your fame beyond the ends of the earth."

On January 2, 1825 the Liberator, disgusted with the criticism circulated against him and the liberating army by representatives of Quito and Guayaquil to the Central Congress of Bogotá, presented his resignation to the Colombian Congress as President of the Republic, saying in part that while the people had overly rewarded his military services with their gratitude, he could bear the enormous weight of the Presidency but "now that the fruits of peace are beginning to intoxicate these same peoples, the time is opportune to move away from the terrifying danger of civilian dissensions to safeguard my only treasure: my reputation. I, therefore, resign for the last time the Presidency of Colombia. I have never exercised it. Accordingly, I will not be missed."

He added that if his country needed a soldier his sword would always be ready to defend it. In this same communication he renounced the 30,000 pesos (dollars) annual pension that had been assigned to him, saying that the depleted Treasury of the Republic needed it more than he.

The Colombian Congress by unanimous vote refused to accept his resignation.

On February 10, 1825, scarcely one year after Bolívar had been appointed Dictator of Peru, he presented his resignation before the assembled Peruvian Congress, saying in part:

"Legislators: Upon restoring to the Congress the Supreme Power vested in me, allow me, with my resignation, to congratulate the people for having, with the victory of Ayacucho, been liberated from what is the most terrible scourge in the world: War and despotism. My destiny as auxiliary soldier compels me to contribute to the liberation of Alto Perú (Upper Perú) and to the surrender of Callao, the last stronghold of the Spanish Empire in America. After completing these tasks, I will rush to my country to render an account to the Colombian Representatives of the people of my mission in Perú, of your liberty, and the glory of the liberating army."

The Peruvian Congress not only did not accept his resignation but awarded him, as an expression of gratitude for his services, the sum of One Million Soles (dollars) and ordered the coining of a medal with the following inscription:

On the obverse: "To its Liberator, Simón Bolívar."
On the reverse: "Perú restored at Ayacucho, Year 1824."

The Peruvian Congress also ordered the erecting of an equestrian statue of the hero to be placed in the Congressional Square of Lima. Another Million Soles was awarded to be distributed by the Liberator among the Generals, Officers and soldiers of the liberating army.

The Liberator, in rejecting the Million Soles awarded to him said in part to the President of the Congress:

"I have never accepted from my own country any reward of this nature. It would therefore be a monstruous inconsistency if I were to receive now from Perú what I have refused from my own fatherland."

As the Peruvian Congress insisted, the Liberator, again refusing the Million Soles, said to its President:

"Excellency: . . . The Congress has named me Father and Saviour of Perú; it has decreed me the honor of Life President; it has ordered the coining of my bust in a medal; it has called me Liberator; it has compelled me to take charge of the Executive Power of Perú, and after all that, it wishes to reward me with an enormous fortune. I have accepted everything with joy except the last gift because the laws of Colombia and those of my heart forbid me."

The Peruvian Congress acceded to his wishes and requested his permission to employ the Million Soles in beneficent works in Colombia. The Liberator agreed to that.

General Sucre was honored by the Peruvian Congress with the illustrious title of "Grand Marshal of Ayacucho" plus an award of 200,000 Soles. Then the Municipality of Lima presented both the Liberator and General Sucre with a gold sword, with their handles studded with diamonds* which they

* The Bolivar Sword is today being exhibited at the Caracas Museum.

received while at Chuquisaca (today: Sucre, Bolivia) on the occasion of the First Anniversary of the Battle of Ayacucho. Colombia, proud of the Liberator's victories in Perú, ordered coined a special platinum medal with the legend:

On the obverse: "Junín and Ayacucho, August 6th and December 9, 1824"

On the reverse: "To Simón Bolívar, Liberator of Colombia and Perú. The Congress of Colombia, 1825."

It also authorized the payment to him of his salaries in arrears, amounting to 150,000 pesos (dollars) which he refused to accept, and never afterward collected. It also restored to the Liberator the extraordinary powers with which he had been previously invested and which had been canceled prior to the Ayacucho victory.

Among the many congratulations and honors the Liberator received from abroad, the United Provinces of the River Plate (Argentina) honored him by sending a special delegation to thank him for his great services to the entire Continent. On this occasion the Argentine Government said to him:

". . . Numerous immortal laurels and palms of victory have been snatched from fortune by the Argentine warriors; but all our trophies appear small before Your Excellency, Sir, the father of five Republics, who has come from the mouths of the Orinoco River from victory to victory, carrying the Iris of Liberty and sealing forever the independence of the New World. The name of Your Excellency is the most precious treasure that the present century will bequeath to the future generations."

These were to be the last days of glory of the Liberator. His sun would soon begin to decline on the not too distant horizon.

CHAPTER X

The Founding of Bolivia

AT THE insistence of the Peruvian Congress, the Liberator agreed to remain in Perú for another year, to mop up the remnants of the Spanish troops under General Olañeta in Upper Perú and to finalize the surrender of the fortress of Callao. Under the terms of the Ayacucho capitulation both Callao and Upper Perú were to be delivered to Bolívar, but their respective Spanish garrisons refused to give up.

The five Provinces of Upper Perú (Bolivia) namely La Paz, Potosí, Chuquisaca, Cochabamba and Santa Cruz then consisted of an area nearly twice the present territory of Bolivia. When Bolivia was first established it had a coast line extending from south of Arica to and including what is today the Chilean port of Antofagasta. This entire coast line was surrendered fifty years later to Chile. The topography of Bolivia can be compared only with that of the Himalayas, in that its territory consists of high Andean snow-capped peaks, and low tropical valleys, thus making communication from one part of the country to the other extremely difficult. Taking advantage of this, each of its neighbors, namely Argentina, Brazil, Chile, Paraguay and Perú seized a section of Bolivian territory during the past one hundred years. Thus Bolivia today is a Mediterranean country similar to Switzerland, without access to the sea.

Upper Perú in 1778 had been separated from the Viceroyalty of Perú and had been placed by the Spanish Government under the direct jurisdiction of Buenos Aires. However, due to the Charcas insurrection of 1809 in Argentina, its five Provinces were again incorporated into Perú, with the result that as both Viceroyalties (Lima and Buenos Aires) had completely neglected Upper Perú, its political status at the time of Bolívar's arrival there was most uncertain.

Bolívar had given instructions to his Lieutenant, General Sucre to limit his intervention in Upper Perú strictly to the military task of liberating the territory from the Spanish yoke and to refrain from interfering in their internal affairs, which could be settled only by the popular free expression of its people with endorsement by the Congresses of both Lima and Buenos Aires. Having received word from the Buenos Aires authorities that they would abide by the wishes of the people of Upper Perú as to their future, the Liberator, from Arequipa, a southern Peruvian city about 770 miles (and thirty days away on horseback from Lima), authorized General Sucre, then at La Paz, to convoke an assembly of representatives of the five Provinces to deliberate on their future. However, Bolívar warned Sucre that any decision of the Assembly was to be submitted to the 1826 Peruvian Congress for ratification.

General Olañeta's Spanish Army in Upper Perú, which prior to Ayacucho was 4600 strong, had suffered the loss of over 50% of its numbers, due to desertions to the patriots' camp as a result of Sucre's army invading that territory. General Olañeta, himself, was killed at Tumusla on April 1, 1825 when he personally tried to suppress an insurrection of some of his remaining battalions. With Olañeta out of the way, the remainder of his troops capitulated and the independence of Upper Perú and that of the rest of South America was consummated.

From Arequipa, Bolívar proceeded to Cuzco, the ancient capital of the Inca Empire, where he remained a month, organizing the local governments and visiting the surrounding territory. It was here, while visiting the Village of Pucará, on August 2nd, that a humble Indian priest, named Choquehuanca, greeted the Liberator with the following eloquent speech:

"God wanted to assemble a powerful Empire of primitive peoples and created (Inca) Manco Capac. The race sinned and the Lord sent Pizarro. After three centuries of atonement, God has had pity on America and created Your Excellency. You are, therefore, the man designated by Providence. None of the previous accomplishments resembles yours, because in order to imitate you, there would have to be created a New World to liberate! You have founded Republics which, in the great development they will achieve, will raise your renown to a height never before attained by man. Your fame will grow as time grows with the course of the centuries and as the shadows grow longer with the setting sun!"

On the 6th of August 1825, the Assembly convoked by Sucre at Chuquisaca declared the independence of the five Provinces of Upper Perú, and named the new State "República Bolívar," later changed to Bolivia. The assembly appointed the Liberator the head of the new Republic during the period of his residence in its territory, and Sucre was placed in charge of its affairs. On the 20th of August, the Assembly proposed that the Liberator draft a Constitution for the new Republic.

Bolívar received the news of the independence of Upper Perú while he was in Puno (Lake Titicaca) and immediately proceeded to La Paz, where he arrived on September 18, 1825. From there he wrote to General Páez at Caracas, ending his letter as follows:

"I am committed to defend Bolivia to the death, like a second Colombia. I am the father of the first and the son of the second. Therefore, my right hand will be in the Mouth of the Orinoco and my left hand will reach the borders of the River Plate. My arms will encompass one thousand leagues (about 3000 miles)."

From La Paz, Bolívar proceeded to Potosí. On October 26, 1825 he addressed his troops on the summit of that silver mountain, saying:

"We have come in triumph from the Atlantic Coast and in fifteen years of gigantic struggle we have destroyed the shackles of tyranny built during three centuries of usurpation and violence. Our joy is immense in seeing so many millions of men restored to their rights by our perseverance and effort. As regards myself, standing on this mound of silver, whose rich veins supplied during three hundred years the Treasury of Spain, I consider this opulence worthless when I compare it with the glory of having victoriously brought the standard of liberty from the torrid sands of the Orinoco to affix it here on the top of this lofty mountain, whose wealth in silver is the amazement and envy of the universe."

As the Year 1825 ended, Bolívar had reached the pinnacle of his glory. He was the arbiter of the destinies of South America, President of Gran Colombia, Supreme Chief of Perú, and President and Protector of Bolivia, ready to send an expedition to Chile under O'Higgins,* who was with Bolívar at the time; besides Bolívar had been asked by the Argentine Government to come and help liberate Uruguay from Brazil; in fact, he was then the man of greatest influence from Mexico to Patagonia.

* O'Higgins, who with San Martín, liberated Chile.

On the 1st of January 1826 the Liberator left Chuquisaca, arriving in Lima on February 7th. Here he received the glad tidings of the surrender of the Callao forts, the commanders of which had capitulated two weeks previously on January 23rd. While at Lima Bolívar again occupied himself with his pet project of organizing a Pan American Congress at Panamá. Two days before the battle of Ayacucho, on December 7, 1824, he had addressed from Lima a communication to the governments of the American Republics, inviting them to send representatives to a Congress to be held at Panamá. In February, 1826, while at Lima, Bolívar wrote a memorandum expounding his ideas on the Panamá Congress, the reading of which, one hundred and forty years later, shows in high relief the genius of his political foresight. We quote here a few paragraphs:

"The relations of the political societies would benefit by a code of law that would rule their universal behavior."

"The New World would be constituted in independent nations, joined together by a common law that would direct their external relations and would offer a conservative power in a general and permanent Congress."

"Internal order would be preserved intact between the various States and within each one of them. None would be considered inferior to the other. None would be the stronger . . . A perfect equilibrium would be established in this new political order. . . ."

"The armies of all would assist the State that would suffer from an external enemy, or from internal subversive factions. . . ."

"The barriers of origin, race and color would disappear."

"In the march of centuries, it is possible that there may

be found only one nation covering the entire world: A Federation."

At Lima, Colonel Mercier, a special envoy sent by the Marquess de Lafayette, presented to him mementos of General Washington, including Washington's portrait sent to Bolívar by Washington's stepson. On March 20, 1826, the Liberator wrote General Lafayette acknowledging the receipt of these priceless objects, saying in part:

"Washington's family honors me in a manner far exceeding my remotest hopes, as a reward from Washington, given by the hand of Lafayette, is the ultimate in human compensation."

And he ended: "What mortal then is deserving of the high honors which Your Excellency and Mount Vernon propose to confer upon me? My embarrassment is equalled only by the infinite sense of gratitude with which I tender to Your Excellency the respect and veneration due the "Nestor" of human freedom." (Nestor was a King of Pylos, who in his old age joined the Greek expedition against Troy, and was noted as a wise counselor.)

On April 2nd the Peruvian Congress and the population of Lima, alarmed with the orders given by Bolívar to General Salom to prepare the return of the troops to Colombia, sent a delegation to La Magdalena, the residence of Bolívar, about three or four miles from Lima, to dissuade him from leaving Perú. When the Liberator agreed, the Congress adjourned its sessions until the following year.

On May 25, 1826, Bolívar submitted his draft of a Constitution for Bolivia to the Congress of that country meeting in Chuquisaca, then its capital. This document, together with the Cartagena Manifest, his Jamaica Letter of September 1815, and his Address to the Congress of Angostura in 1819 constitute perhaps the four major monuments to his philosophy on politics and government. It is regrettable that, due to the abridged nature of this biography, we are unable to publish here this Constitution, having to limit our remarks to a few brief paragraphs of his address to the Bolivian Congress:

". . . Legislators! Your duty compels you to avoid a struggle with two monstruous enemies, who, although they, themselves, are ever locked in mortal combat, will attack you at once. TYRANNY and ANARCHY constitute an immense sea of oppression encircling a tiny island of freedom that is perpetually battered by the forces of the waves and the hurricane that ceaselessly threatens to submerge it. Beware, then, of the sea that you are about to cross in a fragile bark, with so inexperienced a pilot at the helm."

". . . The responsibility of government officials is set forth in the Bolivian Constitution in the most explicit terms. Without responsibility and restraint, the nation becomes a chaos. . . ."

"The most perfect guarantees have been provided for the individual. CIVIL LIBERTY is the one true freedom; the others are nominal or they affect the citizens slightly. The inviolability of the individual—the true purpose of society—and the source of all other safeguards—is guaranteed. PROPERTY RIGHTS will be covered by a civil code, which you should wisely draft in due time for the good of your fellow citizens. I have left intact that law of laws—EQUALITY. Neglect it, and all rights and safeguards will vanish. We must make every sacrifice for it and, at its feet, cast the dishonored and infamous relics of slavery. . . ."

As General José de la Mar, ruling Perú as President of the Council, resigned due to illness, the Liberator appointed in his place General Santa Cruz. This coincided with a military rebellion on July 6, 1826 by two squadrons of Peruvian troops garrisoned at Huancayo. Santa Cruz was compelled to rush there to suppress it. The Peruvian troops, as a pretext for their rebellion, maintained that their purpose was to liberate Perú from Colombian oppression and its soldiers. This event, together with the ominous news he received from Colombia of attempts by Venezuela to secede from Gran Colombia, compelled the Liberator to accelerate his departure from Lima.

Due to objectionable conscription measures against the population of Caracas ordered by General Páez, as Military Commander in Chief of the Venezuelan Provinces, the Bogotá Senate, instigated by Vice President Santander, decreed the suspension of Páez in his military command. The Senate ordered him to appear personally in Bogotá to answer the charges against his command. This Congressional order reached Valencia, a city located about 110 miles west of Caracas, on April 26, 1826. The accusation against Páez before the Bogotá Senate was ill-conceived, and ignored his outstanding services to the Republic, as well as the fact that he was almost worshipped by the Venezuelan people and considered a demigod by his troops.

These Congressional proceedings were kindled by Santander, who was jealous of Páez since the latter had replaced him in command of the patriots' army of the Llanos in 1816. Furthermore, there was a great antagonism between Venezuelans and Neo-Granadians. The Venezuelans resented being dictated to from far-off Bogotá by Santander, a native of Cúcuta (Nueva Granada). Páez was ready to obey the orders of the Central Government but the Municipality and population of Valencia, on April 29th persuaded the General to retain his command.

Páez, after three days of meditation, acceded to the demands of the city, kindled by popular clamor, and ten days later the Municipality of Caracas joined Valencia and reinstated Páez in Supreme Command, not only Military but Civilian, with extraordinary powers to continue until the arrival in Venezuela of the Liberator, President Bolívar.

On the 14th of May, 1826, Páez was sworn into his new official position to uphold the established laws, but with the proviso: *not to obey any orders from the Bogotá Central Government.* Other Provinces in the interior joined Caracas and Valencia and thus, the General Government at Bogotá was repudiated in the Department (political subdivision of Gran Colombia) of Venezuela. This was tantamount to civil war. An Assembly convocated at Valencia for the purpose declared on June 29th that: "the ills afflicting Venezuela were due to the abuses and usurpations with which the Vice President of the Republic, Francisco de Paula Santander has tyrannized the happiness of these inhabitants, the errors of his administration, the easy way with which the fundamental laws lend themselves to assist in the machinations of his revenges."

Páez, from Caracas, wrote the Liberator, who was then in Lima, on May 24, 1826 asking him to accelerate his return to Venezuela "as the people wanted some changes and wanted the Liberator to suggest what they should be." Then, Páez added:

"Everybody considers Your Excellency as his own father, asserting that an illustrious son that has overflowed with glory the greater part of this Continent, should also be the legislator of its own land, after having placed them in full possession of their independence. Without Your Excellency there will be no peace; civil war is inevitable; and if it starts, it will not end until this country is completely destroyed."

Preoccupied with all of these events, the Liberator left Lima on September 3, 1826, after three years in Peru, and embarked at the Port of Callao on the Peruvian warship "Congreso" bound for Guayaquil. On that occasion he issued a proclamation to the Peruvians in which he said:

> "Peruvians:—Colombia is calling me back and I must obey. . . . I am not leaving you. I leave with you my love— in the President and Council of Government, worthy depositories of the Supreme Authority. I leave with you my confidence in the magistrates that govern you; my innermost political thoughts in the draft of the Constitution; and the custody of your independence in the conquerors of Ayacucho. . . ."
>
> "Peruvians:—You have a thousand claims to my heart; I leave it with you forever. Your welfare and your misfortunes will be mine; our destiny will be one."

When the Liberator stepped aboard the war frigate at Callao, he was not aware that the turning point in his career had arrived and that from then on his path would be a calvary of disappointments and bitterness.

Four years later, on the eve of his death, contemplating the work of his life destroyed, the uppermost political accomplishment of his genius—the union of Venezuela, Colombia and Ecuador—crumbling into a heap of ruins, disillusioned and sick in heart and body, he is said to have exclaimed:

"I HAVE PLOUGHED THE SEA!"

CHAPTER XI

The Eclipse of the Sun

D URING the three years spent by the Liberator in Perú, conditions in Colombia had greatly deteriorated. The Province of Pasto had been permanently involved in continuous uprisings. The Southern Departments (Ecuador) during the colonial period were manufacturers of textiles, which were prohibited by Spain to be imported. This industry had been ruined by the Republic, which permitted free importations. Agriculture was practically non-existent because the farmers limited the cultivation of their plantations to providing only for their scanty internal needs, as exporting was unprofitable due to the primitive means of communication. The old taxation system, which during the Spanish regime had been very moderate, was substituted by the Republic with a rather onerous direct tax in 1825. This tax reform was ill-received and was difficult to enforce. As a result, the salaries of civil employees were greatly in arrears and even the army lacked adequate food and supplies.

Nueva Granada was likewise in a semi-bankrupt condition and so was Venezuela due to the freeing of the slaves and the new onerous taxation. Caracas was opposed to having the Executive Powers located in far-off Bogotá, and was also resentful because it considered itself the most highly civilized city of the Republic. This was damaging to the harmony of the country.

This was the situation in Colombia which confronted the Liberator upon his arrival in Guayaquil on September 12, 1826. The Southern Provinces of Ecuador, like those of Venezuela, were against the centralized government of Santander in Bogotá, and were clamoring for reform. It was now claimed that when the Cúcuta Congress first met in 1821 its members, due to the revolutionary war, could not be, and were not the truly elected representatives of the people. It was on this Congress that most of the misfortunes afflicting the Provinces were blamed.

Bolívar at the time was in favor of creating a centralized strong government rather than a Federation because of the chaotic conditions of the country. Then, following the recommendations of the Liberator who was planning to liberate the Southern Provinces of Ecuador, adding them to the union of Venezuela and Nueva Granada, the Cúcuta Legislators nominated Bogotá as the permanent capital of Colombia. Geographically, Bogotá seemed ideal as the Capital because of its central location, midway between the cities of Quito and Caracas. However, what the Congress of Cúcuta tragically overlooked were the difficult means of communication then prevailing, consisting in the main of primitive mule trails over the mountains. This condition made it a task of titans to properly govern and satisfy the needs and welfare of the far-off regions.

Bogotá is located on a plateau, 8600 feet high. To reach this capital city, either from Caracas or Quito, involved a precarious journey, on horseback, requiring the better part of three to four weeks. It was necessary to cross two high ranges of the Andes mountains; if from the north those near Mérida; and if from the south, those between Popayán and the Magdalena River. Besides, there were, particularly in the southern part of the country, numerous torrential mountain streams to be forded, with no bridges then available. Consequently the distant provinces of Ecuador and Venezuela, which under Spanish rule had been accustomed to being autonomously governed by local authorities, felt that under the Republic they had been grossly neglected because they were at the mercy of a remote, hostile ruling body which ignored their most urgent needs.

One of the pet projects of the Liberator at the time was to explore the possibility of a confederation of Colombia with Perú and Bolivia, adopting as their charter the new Bolivian Constitution drafted by Bolívar. To make matters worse, his personal enemies took immediate advantage of these ideas to disseminate, among the dissident population, exaggerated rumors against this new project.

Bolívar remained in Ecuador nearly one month, leaving Quito for Bogotá on October 5, 1826. While on the way to the capital he received at Popayán adverse news from Perú where his enemies had begun to attack him and Colombia. On October 26th from Popayán he sent to General Santa Cruz, President of the Council governing Perú, a communication considered by historians as a masterpiece of statesmanship, unselfishness and self-sacrifice in the interest of the lands he liberated. The Liberator said in his letter that it had become crystal clear to him that the people of Perú wanted to rid themselves of any annoying foreign dependency, and that the will of the people, as the supreme law, should not be opposed. He advised Santa Cruz and the Council of Government to follow the will of the Peruvians, discard the plan for the projected federation of Perú with Colombia and Bolivia, and adopt designs exclusively Peruvian. Referring to the Colombian troops yet in Perú, he ended his letter as follows:

"When the Council of Government may consider that the Colombian troops are a source of embarrassment or are harmful to Perú, it should immediately dispatch them to Colombia, trying to settle part or all of their salaries. If there are no funds available for this in the Peruvian Treasury, the troops will return without pay because we Colombians went to Perú only in quest of glory and brotherhood."

The Liberator arrived at Bogotá on November 14, 1826. But as during his absence his enemies had spread the news that he tried to perpetuate himself in power by becoming a king, on November 23rd, upon assuming the Presidency, he issued a proclamation in which he said:

"Colombians: . . . The ills that afflict you have called me back to Colombia. I arrive full of zest to dedicate myself to the national will; that will be my code because, it being sovereign, it is infallible. The national vote has compelled me to assume command; I abhor it deeply because due to it I am branded as ambitious and desirous of becoming a king. What? Do they consider me such a fool that I aspire to debase myself? Don't they know that the title of Liberator is more sublime than any throne?" And he concluded:

"Colombians! I return to submit myself to the unbearable weight of the executive power, because in times of danger my detachment would be branded as cowardice, not as moderation. Permit me then to serve you as a simple soldier and true republican, as a citizen armed in defense of the beautiful trophies of our victories: YOUR RIGHTS!"

The Liberator left Bogotá for Venezuela, reaching Maracaibo before the end of 1826. While at Maracaibo he issued various decrees and proclamations which created great commotion in the western Provinces, where the mention of his magic name was sufficient to instigate the defection of contingents of troops formerly faithful to General Páez. From

Maracaibo, the Liberator proceeded to Puerto Cabello, where he arrived on December 31, 1826. By this time he had succeeded in bringing into submission under his command half of the Venezuelan Provinces. Meanwhile Páez, who was at nearby Valencia, surrounded by a small detachment of troops and faithful friends, disconcerted with the great number of defections, was deeply moved by the universal popular acclaim and enthusiasm that greeted the Liberator everywhere.

On the following morning, January 1, 1827, Bolívar, abhorring the thought of a bloody and prolonged civil war (because General Páez still had a large following in the llanos), with a master stroke of his statesmanship, issued a decree intended to bring back into the fold of the Republic all of the dissident parties. Briefly the decree said that no one would be prosecuted, judged or punished for his acts, speeches or opinions concerning the reform (meaning secession from the authority of the Central Government); granting the most complete guarantees over the properties and employment of all those involved in the matter of reforms; declaring that General Páez was to continue to exercise the Supreme Civil and Military Authority of Venezuela under the title of "Jefe Superior de Venezuela"; and recognizing General Mariño as General Commandant of the Department of Maturín (Eastern Venezuela); and ordering immediately after the decree was promulgated that the authority of the Liberator as President of the Republic be recognized and obeyed; and that any further hostile act would be considered a crime against the State.

The next day, January 2, 1827, Páez and Bolívar met at the foot of the mountains separating Puerto Cabello from Valencia and peace was restored. On January 10th Bolívar made his triumphal entry into Caracas, together with General

Páez. The latter noted, to his discomfort, that the popular acclaim, the explosion of enthusiasm of the people, was all directed to the Liberator, while Páez was totally ignored. This was the last time Bolívar was destined to pass in life through the streets of the city where he was born. The next time he returned, fifteen years later, was in a coffin, as a corpse, tardily reclaimed by his fellow citizens from a tomb in an alien land.*

After remaining in Caracas six months, during which time he reorganized the various branches of the Administration, particularly the Treasury, the Liberator left for Bogotá, via Cartagena, on July 5, 1827, on board a British warship, which had brought to Venezuela Sir Alexander Cockburn, a special Envoy sent by the British King to congratulate Bolívar. Cockburn, who planned to return immediately to England, offered to take the Liberator and his entourage to Cartagena on the British warship. As the vessel sped on its way westward, skirting the Venezuelan coast. Bolívar looked on that land for the last time: never more was he to see the land, the first of those liberated by him, which was first always in his love. Even as he skirted Venezuela on his way to Cartagena plots were being hatched by Venezuelans against him, plans were maturing which were to bar him forever from her shores.

While on his way overland, from Cartagena to Bogotá, he received news at Ocaña of another revolt in Perú, which had now spread north to Guayaquil. This time it was not only Perú but the third partner of Bolívar's Gran Colombia which was in disorder. Also, while the Liberator had been in Caracas Santander had continued his campaign against Bolívar's popularity with a purpose similar to that of Páez at Caracas: seces-

* The body of the Liberator was repatriated to Caracas in 1842, from Santa Marta, Colombia.

sion of Nueva Granada from Venezuela, trying to undermine the foundations of La Gran Colombia, seeking to displace the gift of liberty given by Bolívar to South America.

Bolívar arrived at Bogotá on September 10, 1827, where the Congress, which had complete confidence in him, immediately ratified all of his Venezuelan measures, confirming at the time his Valencia decree of January 1, 1827, and issued regulations to convoke a General Convention of the Representatives of the three Departments of Gran Colombia, to meet at the City of Ocaña six months later. Furthermore, alarmed over the unfavorable news from Perú, the Congress invested Bolívar with extraordinary powers.

The Liberator remained six months at Bogotá, during which time he maintained a courteous attitude toward Santander avoiding, for the sake of harmony in the Government, the break that was to come later. However, as Santander had been elected a member of the Ocaña Convention and thus could not officiate at the same time as Vice President, Bolívar, using his extraordinary powers, relieved Santander of this Vice Presidency and authorized his Cabinet to assume the executive authority during his own absence from Bogotá.

On March 16, 1828 the Liberator left the Capital for Cartagena, where an abortive revolt had taken place. However, while en route, receiving word that order had been restored there, he stopped at Bucaramanga, remaining there for three months to be near the Ocaña General Convention. The Convention finally met on April 9, 1828 and adjourned two months later on June 19th, with no other tangible results than to show the deep chasm dividing the various political parties, which was soon to result in the dissolution of Gran Colombia.

Gravely concerned over the bickerings against the Liberator at Ocaña, the Governor of the Province of Cundinamarca convoked a popular assembly at Bogotá, at which the members issued a resolution that: "any ruling issued by the Ocaña Convention should not be obeyed, and that the Liberator should assume the Dictatorship of the country, with full powers to convoke Congress when he, in his sole judgment considered it advisable. The Bogotá resolution was subsequently approved by most of the Provinces of the Republic, including the larger cities like Quito, Guayaquil, Cuenca, Panamá Cartagena, Medellín, Popayán, Caracas, Valencia, Cumaná and Maracaibo.

Soon after, on June 24, 1828, Bolívar returned to Bogotá and, confronted with the dangers afflicting Colombia from within, harassed by the recent disturbances in Perú and Bolivia, he, against his wishes, acceded to the popular clamor and reluctantly accepted the Dictatorship, saying on that occasion:

> "The Nation is in danger. I come to its call ready to sacrifice everything for the country. When the people want to deprive me of the power and separate me from the command, I shall gladly submit to their will, and will surrender to them my sword, my blood and my life. This is the sacred oath I utter before all the principal magistrates, and what is more before all the people."

Three days later he issued a decree convoking a Constitutional Congress for 1830 and declaring that in the interim the 1821 Constitution would govern the country. At the same time, making use of his extraordinary powers, the office of Vice President of the Republic was abolished. To compensate Santander for the loss of his office, Bolívar appointed him Colombian Minister to the United States, which Santander immediately accepted, and proposed to take with him to the States as his Secretary, Luís Vargas Tejada, a man who was at the time conspiring to assassinate the Liberator and who, scarcely a few weeks later, nearly succeeded in his Machiavellian plot.

The year 1828 had begun full of forebodings for the young Republic. Early in 1828 the Liberator had been informed of the invasion of Bolivia by Peruvian forces, and as a result of a mutiny of the troops at Chuquisaca on April 18th, General Sucre received several wounds, and his right arm was fractured. Besides the invasion of Bolivia, Perú intended to invade the southern Provinces of Colombia with an army under General Lamar. When Bolívar received word about the invasion of the Ecuador provinces by Perú, on July 25th he issued the following statement:

> "The Government of Colombia goes into this war against its wishes; it does not want a victory stained with American blood; it will try to avoid any armed encounters whenever possible and will always be ready to receive proposals for peace conciliatory with the honor and decorum of the nation over which it presides."

Meanwhile at Bogotá on the night of September 25, 1828 the plot to assassinate Bolívar took place, when the Bolívar Palace was assaulted in a surprise attack by the conspirators, killing several members of the guard, including one of the Liberator's aides-de-camp, Colonel Fergusson. The scheme to murder Bolívar would have been successful but for his presence of mind in escaping through a balcony and the timely arrival of the Vargas battalion, faithful to Bolívar. A military tribunal sentenced fourteen of the conspirators, including Vargas Tejada, to be shot. The latter, however, in trying to escape through the Casanare plains was drowned while attempting to cross a river there. General Santander was also condemned to be shot because of his complicity in the plot but the sentence was later commuted for that of expulsion from the territory of the Republic. While on his way out of the country he was held a prisoner in a dungeon of the Bocachica Fort in Cartagena, and six months later was released and sent into exile. He went to live in Paris.

Returning to the Peruvian invasion of the southern Provinces, the peace so greatly desired by Bolívar was to be settled only on the field of battle. The Peruvian Congress, cognizant of the critical internal situation of Colombia, believed it to be a fine opportunity for Perú to annex to its territory the Colombian southern Provinces, including that of Guayaquil. For this purpose it had sent an expedition of over 4000 troops under General Lamar (later increased to 8400) to the Peruvian northern province of Paita, in order to invade Colombia overland through Asuay. Simultaneously, the Peruvian Navy blocking Guayaquil had succeeded in taking that city.

General Sucre, who after the Bolivian insurrection had resigned his command there and returned to Quito, was appointed by the Liberator as Civil and Military Commander of the three southern Departments, with extraordinary powers to make the peace with Perú. On January 21, 1829, Sucre assumed command of the Colombian troops garrisoned in the three provinces, totaling 4400 men. At the battle of Tarqui, on February 27, 1829, in spite of the Colombians being outnumbered almost two to one, (the Peruvian Army confronting Sucre was 8400 strong) General Sucre inflicted a smashing victory to the enemy. The battle lasted only two hours. The battlefield was strewn with 1500 Peruvian dead. The losses to the enemy were enormous: 2500 casualties in dead, wounded and prisoners, including among the latter 14 high ranking commanders and 60 officers. The Colombian losses were 154 dead and 206 wounded. A generous capitulation granted by

Sucre to Lamar permitted the remnants of the defeated Peruvian Army to withdraw to their country.

When the Liberator received the news of the invasion of southern Colombia by the Peruvians he immediately proceeded to Quito, where he arrived on March 17, 1829. While there he was informed that the Peruvian garrison at Guayaquil refused to surrender the city in accordance with the terms of the capitulation. It took the envoys of the Liberator four months to negotiate an armistice. On July 10, 1829, Guayaquil was finally delivered to the Colombian authorities, and on the 21st Bolívar arrived there. It was while at this city that he became critically ill, with a violent attack of cholera morbus coupled with a high fever. The condition of his health, which had been alarming, had further deteriorated since the assassination attempt of the previous year; also by the continuous calumnies and attacks by the press of the liberated colonies of Spanish America, who questioned the integrity of his intentions and accused him of striving to become a king. It was at this time that he wrote a pamphlet entitled: "Looking over Spanish America," in which when describing the chaos into which those countries were submerged after their liberation from Spain, the impression was given that the Liberator deplored the failure of his work and felt himself responsible for having brought so many misfortunes to the South Americans by leading them to independence.

In a letter to O'Leary, dated September 13, 1829, regarding his illness the Liberator said: "I have suffered a severe bilious attack, which has left me extremely weak and which has convinced me that my vitality is gone forever."

The armistice was followed by a treaty of peace with Perú, signed on September 22, 1829, and immediately thereafter Bolívar left for Bogotá by way of Quito. While on his way to the Capital he received the news of the insurrection of one of his most trusted Generals, José M. Córdova, the hero of Pichincha and Ayacucho. Córdova, disappointed at not having been given the Military Command of the southern Departments and sent instead to Popayán in a secondary position, defected to Antioquia, his native land, where with a handful of followers after taking the City of Medellín, he declared himself in open rebellion against the Central Government. A detachment of veteran troops sent from Bogotá under General O'Leary defeated Córdova's hastily assembled small forces at Rionegro, near Medellín, on October 17, 1829. Córdova was killed in the affray, fighting hand to hand like a lion and refusing to surrender. Bolívar finally arrived at Bogotá on January 15, 1830. His physical appearance was that of a man completely extenuated, ghastly pale; his eyes, which were formerly expressive and full of fire, were now lifeless and listless. His voice was almost inaudible, and his demeanor and carriage indicated that his end was near.

Meanwhile, all of the Provinces of Venezuela, Maracaibo being the last, following the leadership of Caracas confirmed the secession of Venezuela from Colombia. Immediately thereupon, General Páez convoked a Congress to make official this declaration and constitute the new Republic. On hearing this news the Colombian Congress commissioned its President, Sucre, and Vice President, the Bishop of Santa Marta, to go to Caracas and offer peace. When General Páez heard of this mission, he promptly sent his own commissioners to prevent the others from traveling beyond the former borders of Nueva Granada. General Mariño, one of the commissioners, went to the border escorted by a strong contingent of troops with instructions to exact the recognition of the independence of Venezuela. Naturally, Sucre and the bishop, failing in their mission, returned to Bogotá empty-handed.

Due to these distressing developments, the health of the Liberator was visibly losing ground. Insomnia and lack of appetite had practically drained what little was left of his physical and moral strength. Although he was not yet 47 years old, he appeared to be a sexagenarian. In view of the condition of his health he again insisted on resigning but as the Congress then in session claimed that it had been convoked for the specific purpose of improving the Constitution, it considered itself without authority to accept his resignation. Confronted with this impasse the Liberator, on March 1, 1830, using his extraordinary powers appointed General Domingo Caicedo as President of the Council of Ministers in charge of the Executive Power. From that date on the Liberator never again exercised any civil or military commands.

On April 27, 1830, Bolívar reiterated to the Congress his determination not to accept reelection to the Presidency, even if they were to vote for him. To this the President of the Congress answered three days later in a communication which ended as follows:

"Sir: Disregarding what may be the fate that Providence has in store for the Nation or yourself, the Congress expects that all Colombians sensitive to the honor and loving the glory of its fatherland will look upon you with the respect and consideration due the services that you have rendered to the cause of America, and will take care that, preserving always the luster of your name, same may be bestowed upon posterity as is fitting to the founder of the Independence of Colombia."

At the suggestion of Bolívar, Joaquín Mosquera was elected President and General Domingo Caicedo was elected Vice President of the Republic. On May 9, 1830 Congress reaffirmed the life pension to Bolívar of 30,000 Pesos annually as provided in their previous law of July 23, 1823. The Liberator never personally benefited from this pension. He used it to give help to the military and their widows; also for alms to the poor; he gave away all his possessions. Even his country estate outside of Bogotá he gave to a needy friend. The most humble soldier that approached Bolívar never went away empty-handed. He gave away his swords, horses, even some of his finest clothes. He was at the moment penniless. In order to provide himself with some funds for his trip abroad he delivered his silverware to the Mint, receiving for it only 2500 Pesos. By selling his jewels, his remaining horses, etc., he was able to put together for the trip some 17,000 Pesos. He left Bogotá on May 8, 1830 never to return. Becoming seriously ill on the trip to the Coast and after a short stay at Turbaco, he arrived at Cartagena on June 24, 1830. By this time the 17,000 Pesos had diminished to about half due to his munificence in continuously helping the destitute military men who approached him.

It was while he was staying at La Popa, a suburb of Cartagena, that he received news of the assassination of General Sucre, which occurred at Berruecos, near Pasto on June 4, 1830. Sucre at the time was en route from Bogotá to Quito. He was 37 years old. Bolívar, deeply grieved over the loss of his most faithful lieutenant, spent the night pacing back and forth on the cold, clammy La Popa beach. The excessive dampness of the tropical climate was responsible for his contracting a severe cold and fever, which never left him until his death five months later.

To add to his martyrdom the new Congress of Venezuela, convoked by General Páez, meeting at Valencia, sent a communication to the Bogotá Congress informing the latter of the readiness of Venezuela to enter into friendly relations with

Cundinamarca (Colombia) and Quito; but these could not take place, the notification added, while Bolívar remained in Colombian territory. When the Liberator was informed of this, the bitterness of the offense aggravated his illness and accelerated his death. Simultaneously the southern Departments, at an Assembly meeting at Riobamba declared their independence from Colombia under the name of Republic of Ecuador and appointed as its first President one of Bolívar's most trusted lieutenants, General José Flores.

And at Bogotá, on September 2, 1830, an armed revolt deposed the Government and appointed as temporary President, during the absence of Bolívar, General Rafael Urdaneta. Two of the Commissioners sent by Urdaneta promptly arrived at Cartagena to urge the Liberator to return to Bogotá and again assume Supreme Command to save the fatherland. But it was too late—Bolívar was dying.

The Liberator left Cartagena by boat and arrived at Santa Marta on December 1, 1830. He was so weak and in such a complete state of nervous prostration due to the continuous fever, that he had to be carried ashore in a chair. Dr. Alejandro Próspero Reverend, a French physician who was living at Santa Marta, and was Surgeon General of the Military Hospital, took charge of the Liberator. On December 6th, having improved a little Bolívar expressed a desire to be transferred to a country residence. He was transported in a small carriage to San Pedro Alejandrino, a farm about three miles from Santa Marta, near the small Manzanares River, owned by a Spaniard, Joaquín de Mier. On December 10th, with the presentiment that the end was approaching, Bolívar received the last sacraments of the Church and dictated his will. He also issued a proclamation to the Colombians, which was to be his last. Dr. Reverend has left an interesting description of this in his book published in Paris in 1866. He says:

"The Liberator, seated on a bench, surrounded by eight Venezuelan officers, including Generals Silva, Infante, Portocarrero, Carreño and Montilla, began reading this, his last document. However, being overcome with emotion and due to his exhausted condition, he asked Dr. Recuero, the War Auditor, to continue its reading. The Proclamation reads in part:

" 'Santa Marta—December 10, 1830

" 'Colombians: You have witnessed my efforts to establish liberty where tyranny once reigned. I have labored unselfishly, sacrificing my fortune and peace of mind. When I became convinced that you distrusted my motives, I resigned my command. My enemies have played upon your credulity and destroyed what I hold most sacred—my reputation and my love of liberty. I have been the victim of my persecutors, who have brought me to the brink of the grave. I forgive them. . . . I aspire to no other glory than the consolidation of Colombia. . . .

" 'Colombians! My last wishes are for the happiness of our native land. If my death will help to end party strife and to promote national unity, I shall go to my grave in peace.' "

And Dr. Reverend continues: "When Recuero reached the last words: "I shall go to my grave in peace," the Liberator with a hoarse and scarcely audible voice said:

" 'Yes, to my grave . . . that is what my fellow citizens have bestowed on me . . . but I forgive them.' . . . 'I wish I could carry with me the consolation that we all have remained united!' "

On the 17th, Dr. Reverend narrates: "When I noticed that the breathing of the Liberator was difficult, his pulse almost gone, and that the end was imminent, I summoned his Generals, Aides-de-Camp and others of his entourage, saying: 'Gentlemen, if you wish to witness the last moments of the Liberator, this is the time.' "

The Liberator died, according to Dr. Reverend's death certificate, on December 17, 1830, of TUBERCULOSIS. He was 47½ years old. His mother, after bearing four children, of which the Liberator was the youngest, died at the age of 34, also of the same illness: TUBERCULOSIS.

Dr. Reverend, who, after the autopsy and embalming, acted as valet, helping to dress the body of Bolívar, states that as the shirt of the Liberator was in shreds he had to borrow one from General Silva. The veracity of this statement was later attested by the inventory taken of the meager personal effects left by Bolívar at San Pedro Alejandrino—no mention is made of any shirts.

Thus ended the life of the great Liberator, who had done more than any other person since the days of George Washington to bring freedom to the peoples of the Americas.

Simón Bolívar's determination to sacrifice everything to the cause of liberty and his readiness to forgive his detractors in the interest of the most precious goal for which he finally gave his life, have won for him an immortal place in history, a lasting tribute to his greatness.

Appendix

A PORTRAIT OF SIMÓN BOLÍVAR.

SEVERAL members of the British Legion, as well as some of the Venezuelan and Colombian Generals who served under Bolívar, have left us in their Memoirs a fleeting portrait of the Liberator as he appeared to them at that time. We have selected among these the essay written by General O'Leary as perhaps the one that most faithfully describes the salient traits of the Liberator's personality. We copy below a few excerpts from this work:

"Bolívar had a high forehead, slightly narrow, full of furrows since his early youth. Thin, well-shaped eyebrows. A long but perfect nose. Prominent cheekbones, with a notable distance between the nose and the mouth. Well-shaped white teeth. Large but well-proportioned ears. Black wavy hair, on the fine side. Sideburns and moustache, which were eliminated for the first time while he was at Potosí in 1825. He was five feet six inches tall. Narrow chest and thin body and legs. Small feet and hands, whose delicate proportion would have been envied by a woman. His countenance when in good humor was peaceful, but frightening when he was irritated; the change was almost incredible.

"Although he always had a good appetite, he could nevertheless endure hunger better than anyone else. And while he appreciated good food, he partook with relish of the primitive fare of the llanero and Indian soldiers. He was very abstemious; his favorite wines were white wines and champagne, but he never indulged in any of these to excess;

when wine was available, he, personally, filled the glasses of his guests."

"He liked plenty of exercise and I have never known anyone who could endure more hardships. After a strenuous day's journey that would have exhausted the strongest man, he would work for five or six hours or dance as much. He had a passion for dancing.

"He usually slept five or six hours a night, in a hammock, a cot, or on a dry hide on the floor, or wrapped in his cape outdoors, as soundly as if he were on a feather bed.

"In the range of his vision and the fine perception of his hearing, not even the llaneros could surpass him. He was expert in the handling of weapons and an exceedingly skillful and daring rider. Very fond of horses, he, personally, inspected their care while on campaign or in the city and visited the stables several times a day.

"He was most particular about his clothes and scrupulously neat; he took a daily bath, and while in the tropics as many as three baths a day. He preferred the country to the city. Detested drunkards and gamblers but above all liars and gossips. His loyalty and chivalry were such that he never permitted disparaging remarks about others in his presence. Friendship for him was sacred. Trustful to extreme, when detecting deceit he never forgave those who tried to take advantage of his confidence.

"His generosity reached the extreme of lavishness. He not only gave away everything he had, but also incurred debts to help others. While prodigal with his own, he was tight-fisted with the public moneys. He might occasionally have succumbed to flattery, but he abhorred it. He had the rare gift of conversation and liked to narrate anecdotes about his past life. His speeches and writings are replete with daring and original images. His proclamations are models of military eloquence.

"His communications abound in grace, clarity and directness. His military orders to his lieutenants were always issued in the most minute detail; everything was foreseen and thought out in advance. He had the gift of persuasion and knew how to inspire confidence in others. To these qualities were mostly due the amazing victories obtained by him under circumstances so difficult that anyone without these gifts and lacking his perseverance would have failed. An excellent creative genius, he obtained resources where there were none. Always great, he was greater in adversity. A DEFEATED BOLÍVAR WAS MORE TO BE DREADED THAN A VICTORIOUS, commented his enemies. Misfortune made him superior to himself.

"A great judge of men and of the human heart, he appraised at first sight the extent of the capabilities of each one, and very rarely was he proved wrong. He read extensively in spite of the limited time available from his manifold tasks. He spoke and wrote French and Italian fluently. He knew a little English, sufficient to understand what he read. From his studies he was familiar with the Latin and Greek classics, and delighted in reading them in their French translations.

"He greatly disliked the attacks of the press against him, and any slanders irritated him. Although a public figure for twenty years, he never could overcome this touchiness, uncommon in prominent men. He had a high regard for the lofty mission of the press, as censor of public behavior and as a brake to immorality. He attributed the greatness and high moral standards of the British people to the influence of this civilizing agent."

Thus, through the abridged pages of this essay, we have tried to show glimpses of the multiple facets of the life of the Great Liberator, as a warrior, statesman, legislator, and writer —but what is more important as a man, by delving into his human weaknesses and failings, which he was able to master only through the genius of his tenacity and superior judgment.

Bibliography

de Alba, Pedro, "The Democratic Concept of Bolívar," Washington, 1941
Andre, Marius, "Bolívar et la Democratie," Paris, 1924
Angell, Hildegarde, "Simón Bolívar, South American Liberator," New York, 1930
Baralt & Diaz, "Resúmen de la Historia de Venezuela," 3 vols. Curacao, 1887/1893
Bonilla, Manuel C., "Epopeya de la Libertad—Pichincha," Lima, 1922
Brice, Angel Francisco—"Santander Sentenciado por Urdaneta," Caracas, 1948
Cortés Vargas, Carlos, "Participación de Colombia en la Libertad del Peru," 2 vols.
  Bogotá, 1946
Ducoudray-Holstein, H. L. V., "Histoire de Bolívar," Paris, 1831
Francia, Felipe, "Origenes del Gran Mariscal de Ayacucho," Caracas, 1920
Frank, Waldo, "Birth of a World," Cambridge, Mass., 1951
Garcia, Lautico, S.J., "Francisco de Miranda y el Antiguo Régimen," Caracas, 1961
Garcia, Naranjo, Nemesio, "Simón Bolívar," New York, 1931
Lecuna, Vicente, "Cartas del Libertador," 12 vols, Caracas, 1929-1959
—— "Papeles de Bolívar, Caracas," 1917
—— "Proclamas y Discursos del Libertador," Caracas, 1939
—— "Documentos Referentes a la Creación de Bolivia," 3 vols., Caracas, 1924
—— "La Entrevista de Guayaquil," Caracas, 1948
—— "Cartas de Santander," 3 vols., Caracas, 1942
—— "Crónica Razonada de las Guerras de Bolívar," 3 vols, Caracas, 1950
—— "Relaciones Diplomáticas de Bolívar con Chile y Buenos Aires," 2 vols., Caracas,
  1954
—— "Bolívar y el Arte Militar," New York, 1955
—— "Liberación del Perú—Campañas de Junín y Ayacucho," Caracas, 1941
—— "Catálogo de Errores y Calumnias en la Historia de Bolívar," New York, 1956
Lecuna & Bierck, "Selected Writings of Bolívar," 2 vols., New York, 1951
López, Manuel Antonio, "Campaña del Perú," Caracas, 1843
—— "Recuerdos Históricos," Bogotá, 1878
López Contreras, Eleázar, "Synopsis of the Military Life of Sucre," New York, 1942
—— "Bolívar, Conductor deTropas," Caracas, 1939
—— "El Pensamiento de Bolívar Libertador," Caracas, 1950
Ludwig, Emil, "Bolívar," New York, 1942
Mancini, J., "Bolívar," Paris, 1914
Monsalve, Juan de Dios, "El Ideal Político del Libertador," 2 vols., Madrid, 1916
Montilla, José Abel, "Bolívar y la Gran Colombia," México, 1935
O'Leary, Daniel F., "Bolívar y la Emancipación de Sud América, Narración" 3 vols.,
  Madrid, 1951
—— "Correspondencia," 12 vols., Caracas, 1879/1880
—— "Documentos," 14 vols., Caracas, 1881/1884
Olivas Escudero, Obispo Fidel, "Apuntes para la Historia de Huamanga," Ayacucho,
  1924
Páez, José Antonio, "Autobiografía," 2 vols., New York, 1945
Parra Perez, C., "Bolívar, His Political Ideas," Paris, 1928
—— "Miranda et la Revolution Francaise," Paris, 1925
Pérez Vila, Manuel, "Vida de Daniel F. O'Leary," Caracas, 1957
Porras Troconis, Gabriel, "Campañas Bolivarianas de la Libertad," Caracas, 1953
Posada Gutiérrez, Joaquín, "Ultimos Días de la Gran Colombia y del Libertador," 3 vols.,
  Madrid, 1920
Restrepo, José Manuel, "Historia de la Revolución de la República de Colombia," 4 vols.,
  Besançon, France, 1858
Reverend, Alejandro Próspero, Dr., "La Ultima Enfermedad, Los Ultimos Momentos
  y los Funerales de Simón Bolívar," Paris, 1866
Robertson, William S., "The Life of Miranda," University of North Carolina, 2 vols.,
  1929
Rodríguez Villa, "El Teniente General Don Pablo Morillo," 4 vols., Madrid, 1910
Romero, Carlos, "La Campaña de Ayacucho Después de Junín," Lima, 1924
Rourke, Thomas, "Man of Glory—Simón Bolívar," New York, 1939
Santana, Col. Arturo, "La Campaña de Carabobo," Caracas, 1921
Sardi, José Nucete, "Aventura y Tragedia deDon Francisco de Miranda," Caracas, 1956
Sherwell, Guillermo A., "Simón Bolívar," Clinton, Mass., 1951
Sociedad Bolivariana de Venezuela, "Decretos del Libertador," 3 vols., Caracas 1961
Trend, J. B., "Bolívar and the Independence of Spanish America," Clinton, Mass., 1951
Union Panamericana, "Centenario de Ayacucho," Washington, 1924
Valdés, Gerónimo, "Refutación al Diario de Sepúlveda," Vitoria, Spain, 1827

147

Vaucaire, Michel, "Bolívar the Liberator," Cambridge, Mass., 1929
Yáñez, Francisco Javier, "Relación Documentada—Venezuela Hasta 1821," 2 vols., Caracas, 1943
——— "Compendio de la Historia de Venezuela," Caracas, 1941
Yáñez, Germán G., "Ultima Campaña de la Independencia del Perú," Lima, 1924
Ybarra, Thomas R., "Bolívar the Passionate Warrior," New York, 1929